D1088727

BELUE TO SCOTT!

The greatest moment in Georgia football history

GOD Bless + Go Dawgs,

Robbie B

Jer. 29:11

BELUE TO SCOTT!

The greatest moment in Georgia football history

BY ROBBIE BURNS • FOREWORD BY LARRY MUNSON

© 2010 Robbie Burns

Edited by Freddy Jones and Buddy Sullivan
Cover and page design by Garon Hart Graphic Design
Cover photos by Wingate Downs and Perry McIntyre

Printed in U.S.A.

ISBN 978-0-615-39400-8

Quantity discounts available for your organization.
For further information, contact:
H&H Publishing Company
Macon, Ga.
rdburns00@aol.com

www.beluetoscott.com

Contents

Foreword

The Georgia-Florida game was still pretty new to me. Before coming to Georgia in 1966, I was not aware of it at all. Year after year, the series and the games were getting bigger and bigger, or so it seemed. There was more conversation about it. People were snarling and snapping, but I did not realize, I don't think, how much it meant for the two schools. I did not recognize how much it meant to Florida that they were losing, and quite often tough, tough football games. Close games.

It was a very big series, and it became more and more difficult. It was a bowl atmosphere. There's no doubt about that. There were some finishes in almost every Georgia-Florida game where somebody won it close, right near the end. As the years went on, I think we were seeing the deep feelings between the two schools. The Florida people were more and more outspoken about losing the game or even playing Georgia. I think the thing was almost getting out of hand before the play happened.

The play was almost like slow motion. It seemed like the game was over, and as the play unfolded, all of us had just about given it up. We had the ball, and we were down on our own seven or something like that. Here comes a play, and here comes Buck trying to pass to one man. We didn't have any idea what pattern they had called. Again, it seemed like slow motion because we got in trouble behind the line for just a second or two. Then, big number 65, Nat Hudson, stood up and blocked with one shoulder. He nudged, just nudged some guy out of the way who was about to take Buck down.

I happened to see number 65 on him and mentioned something like Buck's in trouble. That's about all I got out of my mouth, but I could see that somebody was protecting him, and that's when he threw the ball. Now, there was a little bit of luck after that because Florida had a couple of defensive backs that slipped. We were lucky to complete the play. Without that lineman standing up and spotting somebody coming in, we would not have completed it.

I wasn't aware of the impact the call of that play had. I didn't give it any thought, not for quite a while. All of a sudden, people were calling from all over, and they wanted a copy of the play. They were playing it on their morning shows. People used to ask about the play all the time. You couldn't go to any quarterback club without people wanting to talk about it. If Lindsay Scott was on the program with you, there was a lot of discussion about the play. At first, you didn't look at it like the play of the season or the play of the years. It was just a helluva play that happened.

It was a moment of triumph, and then, as the years went on, there were more and more repercussions off the play. Lindsay Scott couldn't walk down the streets from Jesup to Americus to anywhere. He said he would park his car and people were hollering across the street, and said they still do, 'Lindsay Scott, Lindsay Scott, Lindsay Scott.' He said that play had meant everything to him. The play helped to define, for a while, Georgia football. As it turned out, we won a championship with it.

Larry Munson

Acknowledgements

To acknowledge anyone but Jesus Christ first would be turning my back on the One who has made all this possible. Everyone else that will be mentioned below is because my Lord sought to bring them into my life for many reasons, and one of them was this book. He promises a plan for my life (Jeremiah 29:11), and 43 years into it, I can look back see so much of it to this point. So, He truly is the genesis of every element in the journey of writing *Belue to Scott!*

I cannot think of traveling this road without my wife, Dawn, son, Hunter and daughter, Hannah Rose. Dawn has been ultra supportive during my times of doubt and confidence, and I know she has prayed for me every day over the last 20 months. I love her so much for all that and more. Hunter and Hannah Rose have been extremely patient and understanding with my "lack of sleep" and hearing me say, "I'm working on the book tonight." I love you both!

The people that planted the seeds for this book over three decades ago are my mom and dad. As a kid, I was a Georgia fanatic, and they, along with my sister, Debbie, endured every autumn as I literally lived and died with my heroes in Red and Black. I began to tape the broadcasts off the radio in 1978 and my parents supported and encouraged this passion with the purchase of countless cassette tapes I would use each Saturday.

They also allowed me to hoard numerous college football magazines and newspaper clippings. Thirty years later, I still have most of these items, and they have been used as research material to write this book. Without my parent's blessing then, that childhood passion might not still burn today. Thank you mama and daddy...I love you!

No writer can go without thanking their high school English teachers. I had two great ones at Tattnall Square Academy in Pat Jenkins and Doe Watson. They both encouraged me to write and made sure I did it correctly. Both spilled a lot of red ink on my papers, and I'm very grateful for it.

After graduating from Mercer University, I enjoyed a great internship at Louisiana State University in its sports information office. One of the first things I did was ask my boss, Herb Vincent, if I could dig through the rich and storied history of LSU athletics. He agreed and for the next three years, I worked closely with Bill Franques writing historical pieces for the football and basketball game programs. Herb and Bill played a critical role in where I am today, and I can't thank them enough for the opportunity.

A great deal of gratitude goes to my bosses at the Georgia Sports Hall of Fame. For 11 years, Med Park, Bob Callaway, Alice Knierim, John Shafer and Jackie Decell fanned the flames of my passion for the history of sports in Georgia and let me research to my heart's content. It is there, I also learned of the many different angles to historic events from our curator, Alan Robison, and the multitude of stories that are found in each. This book was certainly born from the lessons I learned and leadership I received there.

I had no idea how to write a book, so I had to lean on those who did. There's no telling where I would be without established authors like Bert Sugar, Tony Barnhart, Ed Grisamore, Jackie K. Cooper, Joe McDaniel and Sydney Matthews. Bert is one of the greatest and most highly regarded sports historians to ever live. I'm blessed to have met him while working at the Georgia Sports Hall of Fame, and so thankful this member of the World Boxing Hall of Fame would help a first-timer like me.

Tony is THE guru of college football and being a Bulldog himself did not hesitate when I called. Thanks so much, Tony! Ed took me to lunch and mapped out many of the pitfalls and potholes I needed to keep watch for. I still owe you lunch when

I reach that certain number of books sold! I count these six men as dear friends. Their wisdom, knowledge, and personal experiences helped readied me for the unknown.

Without Jami Gaudet, the flow of this book would be very different. Jami is a respected author in her own right, and her attention to detail is meticulous. She took my original thoughts on the book and gave them new life, shaping it into something much more dynamic.

I needed seasoned writers to serve as editors, and thankfully, Freddy Jones and Buddy Sullivan agreed. Both men covered the 1980 Georgia-Florida game for The Macon Telegraph and Lagrange Daily news, respectively, so I knew they would offer editorial and historical expertise at the same time. They did exactly that!

The sports information departments at Georgia and Florida were invaluable with their assistance. Norm Carlson and Steve McClain at Florida were extremely open to help on an event that is not fondly remembered by Gator fans. I greatly appreciate them. Georgia's Claude Felton is simply the best! A friend and mentor to me, the Hall of Famer handled every inquiry I presented with the patience of Job, and there were many. It's my honor to have Claude involved with this.

Many thanks to Mary Linneman at Georgia's Hargrett Library and the many librarians contacted throughout the Peach State and Florida. This could not have been thoroughly researched without the help of these resources: *The Macon Telegraph, The Atlanta Journal-Constitution, The Athens Banner-Herald, The Florida Times Union, Sports Illustrated, Street and Smith's 1980 Official College Football Yearbook, The Evening Independent, The St. Petersburg Times, The Ocala Star-Banner, The Post, The Rome News Tribune, Gainesville Sun, The New York Times, The Savannah Morning News, The Augusta Chronicle, Daytona Beach Sunday News Journal, Sarasota Herald Tribune, The Lakeland Ledger, USA Today, The Red & Black, Hunker Down!, Glory Yards, 100 years of Georgia Football 1882-1992, and Georgia vs. Florida, War Between The States.*

The information would be nothing without the pictures that complement it so well. Thanks to Bobby Haven, Wingate Downs, Perry McIntyre, Randy Miller, William Winburn and Fred Bennett for capturing this historic moment.

To Garon Hart, the designer of *Belue to Scott!* I asked the Lord to bring me a great book designer and one who was honest, ethical and easy to work with. That would be Garon. Not only is he great at his craft, but he is a great person!

I cannot thank my many relatives and friends who have lifted this project up in prayer from its inception nearly two years ago. Debbie, Annie, Caroline, Rick, Jimmy, Danny, Brad, April, Henry, Stacey, Tim, Jay, Bobby and others, thank you being part of my "focus group" and for supporting this while on your knees.

This classic game would not be nearly as special if not for the voice of my youth, Georgia's legendary Larry Munson. His call is remembered as much as the play itself and still brings all Bulldogs to their feet. To have you handle the foreword is a personal honor I will never be able to thoroughly express.

To the 1980 Georgia and Florida teams, thank you for taking the time to share your memories, both good and bad. It especially took a lot of guts for the Florida coaches and players to revisit this, and I respect each of them for it. This book has provided me with a new respect for what took place that day in the Gator Bowl and what *Belue to Scott!* really means.

Robbie Burns

Introduction

It was the defining moment for a generation of Georgia Bulldog fans. You remember where you were and what you were doing as Buck Belue eluded disaster and Lindsay Scott bolted into Georgia gridiron lore.

That one play and one moment have been passed down over the last three decades like a priceless family heirloom. The memories are willed to younger fans, who were not even born, so the thread of that moment might never be broken.

It was a day I will never forget. As a ninth-grader, I remember bursting from my room and running laps through the den, kitchen and living room, enveloped in shear delight. My dad, 1958 Georgia alumni, sat in his chair in disbelief knowing Georgia was very fortunate to have dodged the deadliest of pigskin bullets.

In 1980, I taped each Georgia game off the radio. From home, I played Larry Munson's highlights back to the middle Georgia community on WMAZ radio's Budweiser Scoreboard. Usually, I would then head down the street and meet up with my "big brothers", Danny Morton and Jimmy Waite, to play ball at the Salt Palace.

On November 8, 1980, I never made it. I replayed Munson's classic call numerous times to the listening audience. Our phone rang long into the evening with Bulldog fans, including my Uncle Dean from Atlanta, requesting a playback of "Lindsay Scott! Lindsay Scott! Lindsay Scott!" via Ma Bell.

Three decades later, Munson's extolling of "Run Lindsay" is as fresh as a Peach pulled from the tree. This book is an attempt to look at the greatest play and greatest moment in Georgia football history from every possible angle and through the eyes of numerous people in many different situations when the act occurred.

I will never look at this play and game the same again. After reading this book, I hope the same will be true for you.

GOD Bless and Go Dawgs,
Robbie Burns

To the King of the Universe,
my Lord and Savior JESUS CHRIST.
Without Him, this book could have
never been written.

1 Blood and Guts

It is more than a football game. The Georgia-Florida rivalry is a signature event on almost every fan's yearly calendar. It is so important, it ranks in the top five with Christmas, Thanksgiving, Easter and summer vacation. The game is such a happening that weddings are rescheduled around this weekend to insure friends, loved ones and even the bride and groom themselves will be in attendance. I know first-hand. Mine was rescheduled one week after the 2000 contest.

Who would have known in 1904 at Central City Park in Macon, Ga., site of the series' first game, that it would grow into such a cultural event. Since 1933, regardless of the records, circumstances or situations, it has beckoned the faithful from each institution to make the annual pilgrimage to Jacksonville just as birds fly south every winter.

Like a perfect sauce - or better yet for the Georgia-Florida game - the perfect drink, it contains all the right ingredients: atmosphere, intensity, importance and indelible moments.

Julie Moran, who later became a groundbreaking sports journalist with ABC Sports, sat in the Gator Bowl for many of these late fall clashes as a child. Her grandfather, Sterling "The Duke" Dupree, coached most of his career at Georgia but during a brief stint at Florida, he recruited the Gators' first Heisman winner, Steve Spurrier. From her view, the rivalry was unlike anything she has ever seen.

"It wasn't like being in Athens," Moran remembered. "It wasn't like being at any other game. It was just some type of kinetic energy that went on in that stadium. I can't describe it and it never was duplicated at any other college football game I ever saw or worked on.

"For many years, I was the sideline reporter with Brent Musburger and Dick Vermeil. That stadium, that game is still at the top of my list, and I went all over...Penn State, Ohio State, and I went to the Rose Bowl. It probably has a lot to do with my background, but something about that game, that stadium looking out over that one end zone over the water. It had a lot of....I don't know...what's the word....I can't even think of the word...it was just kind of surreal in a way."

Georgia alumnus Greg McGarity worked for the Georgia athletic department from 1979-1992, and at Florida the next 18 years as an associate athletic director. He returned to Georgia as its new athletic director in 2010. As a student at Georgia, he said the game "was the highlight of the year." The weekend itself was, and still is a diversion from the norm.

Greg McGarity

"It gave the Georgia students and season ticket holders a chance to escape and get into the state of Florida," he said. "The weather was always like you would imagine Florida weather would be. It was usually short sleeve shirt weather and beautiful that time of the year. It was a trip where everybody took a couple of days off and went to Jekyll Island, Sea Island, Brunswick or down into Jacksonville and stayed and had a great time."

The game is also serious business. For the fans, it is an imbedded loyalty and passion that has been passed down for generations.

"I grew up in Folkston (Georgia) which is right on the Georgia-Florida line and only 40 miles from Jacksonville," said Freddy Jones, who covered the 1980 game for The Macon Telegraph. "I went to my first Georgia-Florida game when I was 10 years old and attended over 40 plus in a row. That was just a way of life. If you grew up in South Georgia, you learned at a very early age your feelings toward Florida."

For the players, it is an "x" that marks the spot on their football calendar.

"There were two games every year that when you worked out in the summer, you thought about who you were getting ready for," said Robin Fisher, Florida's starting nose guard in 1980. "That was the Florida-Florida State game and the Georgia-Florida game. No doubt about it. Those two games registered as the big pay days that we worked all year for. One gave you state bragging rights. If you didn't get through Georgia you probably weren't going to get through the SEC very well."

Legendary SEC referee Bobby Gaston said no other rivalry game he worked could match the "feelings" these players share. He was involved in many of the South's most intense gridiron grudge matches

such as Mississippi-Mississippi State, Tennessee-Alabama and Alabama-Auburn.

"The Georgia-Florida guys don't like each other," he said. "You just don't sense that with some of these other rivalries. Alabama-Auburn guys are basically from the same state and even though the rivalry is intense, there's not as much intensity on the field as there is with the Georgia-Florida game. It's hard to separate it and tell you how or why, but you just feel like the Georgia-Florida series is a little bit more than all of them I've worked."

The intensity of the late season meeting was always heightened by the ramifications on the winner and the loser.

"For Florida, if you got past the Georgia game, the only league games we had left to play were Kentucky and Vanderbilt," McGarity said. "Just like Georgia had to get past Auburn. It was always the pivotal game of the year if you were going to be SEC champion."

Before the 1980 meeting, St. Petersburg Times sports writer Ron Martz detailed why the game held such meaning:

"In the 47 years Florida has engaged in SEC warfare, it, has never been able to sit atop the heap at season's end. And Georgia has been one of the main culprits in denying Florida that spot. Every time

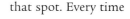

Legendary SEC referee Bobby Gaston shown here in the 1964 Georgia-Florida game when Bobby Etter scored an unlikely touchdown.

Georgia blasted Florida, 51-0, in 1968.

it looks like the Gators are about to claim their first conference championship, they run into Georgia in Jacksonville.

"Five times Florida and Georgia have met with the SEC title, or a share of it, at stake. Five times Florida has lost. And on three of those occasions (1966, 1968 and 1976), Georgia went on to claim the conference championship...In the past, when it came down to Florida-Georgia with SEC spoils to the victor, the spoils have always gone to the 'Dogs."

That was true during Mike Shanahan's four-year tenure (1980-83) as Florida's offensive coordinator. Shanahan has become one of pro football's most respected coaches and influential offensive minds while guiding the Denver Broncos to a pair of Super Bowl titles. Still, the importance of those meetings along the St. Johns River lingers three decades later.

"The only thing I can remember to this day is I am 0-4 against Georgia," he recalled. "That thing still sits in my mind. You go back to the four years I was there, and we didn't beat them one time."

Joe Jackson's first encounter in the Gator Bowl was much different than Shanahan's and produced a cherished, childhood memory.

"My first Georgia Florida game was in 1975," he said. "I was eight and my daddy took me. I lived in Folkston and it was just an hour away from Jacksonville. My mama and daddy had been going for years, back when people would wear suits to the game.

"The thing I remember is daddy saying, 'We better go to beat the crowd' because it was at the end of the game," he said. "At that time, Georgia was getting beat. As we were walking outside, we heard a roar. I remember daddy looking down at me and saying, 'I guess Florida scored again.' We walked a little further and there was a vendor. Daddy asked, 'What just happened?' They guy had a little radio and said, 'Georgia scored.' I went crazy. That was my introduction to Georgia football, Appleby to Washington."

Barbara Dooley warmly remembers the 1966 game when Florida quarterback Steve Spurrier became closely acquainted with Bill Stanfill and Erk Russell's defense.

"We knocked Florida out of many championships," she said. "I'll never forget when Spurrier was up for the Heisman. Before the game, he was walking up and down the sidelines getting his picture made. He was really strutting around. We kept him on his tail the whole day. At that point, I think Spurrier really hated us. To this day, and Spurrier is a friend of ours now, I don't think he'll ever get over the humiliation he took the day we just beat the fool out of them."

ATMOSPHERE

Vince Dooley, former Georgia head football coach/athletic director

"I knew the uniqueness of it going all the way back to when I was a scout at Auburn. I scouted that game eight straight years. There were two places I enjoyed scouting games. One was Baton Rouge when LSU would play Georgia Tech. The other was at Jacksonville because I had a chance to go to either the Florida breakfast or the Georgia bar-b-que or vice versa. There was just a unique atmosphere. It was a fun game to scout."

Frank Ros, Georgia linebacker

"Don't ask me why I remember this, but as soon as you go to the tunnel opening, it was like walking into a cloud of Bourbon vapor. I will never forget that."

Frank Ros

Hubert Mizell, former sports editor
St. Petersburg Times

"Our first house was two blocks from the Gator Bowl stadium. I saw the Bulldogs and Gators play for the first time when I was in junior high. Wally Butts was coaching the Bulldogs at that time. I sold soft drinks and being a Baptist kid, I was a little surprised that Ginger Ale and 7-Up outsold Cokes and Pepsi's. I hadn't figured out it had something to do with those flasks that people had in their coat pockets."

INTENSITY

Mike Shanahan, Florida offensive
coordinator, 1980-1983

"I think everybody just knew growing up what a big rivalry it was, but you don't really know it until you get there and you're a part of it. How important it is to the alumni, to your players and to the university itself. People talk about different types of rivalries; you talk about Michigan, you talk about Ohio State. You get Texas and Oklahoma. At least from my perspective, that (Florida-Georgia) was as good as it was."

Julie Moran, '84 Georgia alumnus

"The rivalry is so intense. It felt a little bit scary walking through that parking lot especially if you won the game. The Florida fans were really upset. That walk back to the car, you were walking on egg shells a little bit. Even before the game, you could watch some of the fans kind of pushing each other's buttons.

Walking into the stadium, I remember a little bit more animosity than any other game."

Hubert Mizell, former sports editor
St. Petersburg Times

"Ohio State-Michigan is enormous—emotionally, athletically, historically. Millions will say there is no college football rivalry more prodigious than Texas-Oklahoma. There will be votes for Stanford-California, Army-Navy, Notre Dame-Southern California and other squabbles of renown.

"But for extreme passions, state-against-state pride and flavor as unique as it is yummy, I say "The King" (in fairness, we'll list university names alphabetically) is Florida-Georgia. A Jacksonville joy of autumn, in a stadium half-stacked with Red and Black zealots, equally loaded with Orange and Blue and totally crazy."

Joe Jackson, Georgia fan

"A lot of Florida fans seem to think Florida football started in 1990. They fail to forget the other years when they were basically a dumb Vanderbilt."

Barbara Dooley, wife of former Georgia
head football coach Vince Dooley

"The rivalry is intense, very intense. When Vince was coaching and we were in control of Florida, the Florida people hated us, just really hated us. I think we kind of laughed and thought, 'We just own them', and got a little cocky. I don't think Florida has ever forgiven us for those years."

Mike Bugar, Florida defensive line coach, 1980-1982

"I think it's one of the best rivalries in college football. Blood and guts. Hell yeah. Let me tell you something, I was recruiting an offensive lineman in Fitzgerald, Ga., and went to a high school basketball game he was playing in. I parked my car and backed it into a spot by the gym. Wayne McDuffie was the offensive line coach at Georgia, and he and I played together at Florida State. McDuffie is inside with some Georgia people, and he sees me walk in. I'm watching the game and I know they're looking at me. They don't say anything to me. The game finishes and I get up and leave. I go out to my car, but I can't see out the windshield. I thought there was some dew on it, and I turn the wipers on and damn glass is flying all over the place. Somebody had taken a rock and threw it at my windshield and cracked and smashed it all up. Now, did somebody from Georgia do it? I don't know. I'm not saying that. My car was backed in where they could not see the Florida license tag. There was nothing on the front of the car to say it was from the University of Florida. The next day, I had to drive all the way to St. Augustine, Fl., looking out the window because I can't see anything with all the glass broken. But, that's the way the rivalry is in recruiting as well as on the field. Blood and guts."

IMPORTANCE

Jimmy Womack, Georgia fullback

"It sounds so immature right now, but I really didn't consider going to Florida because of the colors of the school. Northside High School, that was Warner Robins High School's biggest rival, wore orange and blue. To wear orange and blue, that was a bit much for me. From the time I started playing football, I always wore red and white or red and black. I never knew any other color uniform in my entire career. When I played midget league, we wore white and black. That was the only reason I didn't truly consider Auburn or Florida because they had good programs."

Hubert Mizell, former sports editor St. Petersburg Times

"When I became sports editor of the St. Petersburg Times, it was dedicated to becoming one of the top 10 newspapers in the country. That allowed me to go to great events. I was lucky enough to cover 32 Super Bowls, 10 Olympic games, 30 NCAA basketball final fours, 41 straight Masters golf tournaments, 25 World Series, nine Wimbledon tournaments and a tremendous number of (college football) bowl games. I pretty much saw it all repeatedly. At that time, I didn't know much about the world and Georgia – Florida was as big as it got."

INDELIBLE MEMORIES

Tony Barnhart, CBS Sports

"There were two plays in the Georgia-Florida rivalry I really wish I could have been there for. 1980 was certainly one of them and the other one was in 1975 when I was a student at Georgia. I was working for *The Red & Black*, and I had not been working for them that long. I forget who went down there for us, but I stayed behind in Athens. Me and about eight million other people went to a place called the Fifth Quarter Lounge on the Atlanta Highway. They had one of the original 75-inch big screen TVs. We're sitting there watching the game but can't hear a thing that's going on. When (Richard) Appleby threw the ball to (Gene) Washington, we just about tore that place down."

"Open my eyes"
Joe Creamons, Georgia defensive guard

"What the game meant? I was born in 1959 and raised in Eustis, Fla. about an hour and a half from Gainesville, Fla. My father attended the University of Florida (UF) and parts of my family had been in the state of Florida since 1832. I went to my first Georgia-Florida game in 1971 at the age of 12 and went to Jax (Jacksonville) every year after until the 1976 game, my senior year at Eustis High School. Prior to 1971, I listened on the radio or had watched every game as far back as the mid 1960s. All these years, I was an avid Gator fan.

"When I was in eighth grade, three Eustis players signed scholarships to play with UF. I knew all three well and as I ended my junior year at Eustis and started attracting recruiters, I saw two of them one day. Both told me to 'Open my eyes' during the recruiting process in the fall of 1976. So I did, and took official visits to all in-state schools (UF, Florida State, Miami). My official visit to Georgia (UGA) was the 1976 Alabama game when UGA won 21-0 and also won the SEC title that year. As a defensive lineman, I was absolutely impressed with Erk (Russell), meeting him for the first time and knowing I would play for him. The next morning after the game, we had a coach/recruit breakfast and Coach Russell offered me a scholarship. I committed on the spot!

"On the eight hour drive back to central Florida that Sunday, my dad asked me how the breakfast had gone. When I told him I was offered a scholarship and accepted on the spot, he almost wrecked the car and would not speak to me for three months. Four years later, after the Sugar Bowl game against Notre Dame, I was sitting in the Hyatt hotel in New Orleans with my dad and grandfather drinking a beer. My dad looked at me and said 'Son, I am really sorry for being mad at you back in 1976 for picking Georgia over Florida...you made the right decision.' It took four years, but I finally got an apology!

"By that time (November 1976), I had offers from FSU and Miami, but not UF. Signing day was only a month or so away. Back then, you were able to sign your letter of intent the first of December. The following week I got a call from Florida's defensive back coach, Ken Hatfield, who was recruiting me. He had found out I had 'committed' to UGA and offered me a scholarship over the phone. I stuck with UGA!

"So, the moral of this story is the UF game meant everything to me. Eustis, Fla. was a hotbed for Gator football, and I had bucked UF for UGA. Not a lot of folks in Eustis were happy when I came home every summer. I even worked out with a couple of local guys I had played against in high school that were now playing for Florida. It was even more important to me that we annually beat the Gators. We lost to them my freshman year (1977) and beat them in 1978 when I red-shirted. I am blessed to have played and won three times (1979-1981) in the Gator Bowl against a rival I soon learned to hate."

Tim Groves, Florida safety

"I was at the 1976 game as a senior in high school when we were up 27-13 at half time, and we loose 41-27. It seemed like we had faster guys, a little bit bigger at the time, but they somehow found a way to win the game. When (Vince) Dooley was there, he out-coached us numerous times."

Joe Happe, Georgia center

"What really stuck out was the '76 game when Florida was loaded with all that talent and they were up 27-13 at the half. Georgia had Ray Goff, Matt Robinson. Ray Goff had an unbelievable second half to carry the team. That left a huge impression on me watching that game. I was really, really impressed with Georgia after that."

Hubert Mizell, former sports editor
St. Petersburg Times

"One of the captivating things about this rivalry is it's never been win one, lose one. It's been a streak of domination. Georgia almost never lost to Florida until the 1950s. When Bob Woodruff became the coach at Florida, he brought them up to fairly even terms. Florida was pretty good right on through Ray Graves' time in the 60s, but many of those teams in the 60s and 70s were under achieving.

"It was that way until Vince Dooley was hired at the University of Georgia. He became the dominant factor for more than 20 years. Dooley had a wonderful grip on that series. I always thought Vince had an intellectual way about him. He was a well read man, and he managed to figure things out. I had great respect for him."

Frank Tilton, former sports editor
Savannah Morning News

"It was a great rivalry. I had been at games there when anything could happen. In 1967, Richard Trapp of Florida caught a pass, raced in and turned the whole game around. In 1969, it ended in a tie where one of the teams kicked a field goal and an official had called time. The field goal was missed and the play was done over. Then the field goal was made. Florida was way ahead in 1976 and got real cocky. In the third quarter, they went for it on fourth and one from their own 28. Johnny Henderson came up on a pitch and turned the Florida guy (Earl Carr) upside down for no gain. Georgia took over and Florida never scored again."

Buddy Sullivan, former sports editor
Lagrange Daily News

"I think that's why the older generation of Florida fans take such pleasure in their recent domination in the series because Georgia had broken their hearts so many times. Anytime Florida would have a pretty decent season, Georgia could be just an average team, but Vince Dooley would find a way to beat them and ruin it. There was a history of that with him as the coach."

Bulldogs going for the BIG ONE

By Patrick Zier
The Ledger, Nov. 6, 1980

"There have been some frustrating Gator defeats in this series, but none more vividly illustrates the dominance of their neighbors from the north than the 1976 game.

"The stakes were high in that one too. Both teams were chasing a conference championship, and the winner of this game was to be the champion, and surely it seemed, Florida was to be the winner.

"At halftime, the Gators led, 27-13. Then, in a shocking sequence of events, a fourth down gamble failed and suddenly, it was all turned around. When it was over, the stunned Gators walked off 41-27 losers, and Georgia walked off with another SEC title. That kind of play has been characteristic of the Bulldogs under Dooley. If you could use only one word to describe Georgia during the Dooley era, the word would be tenacious."

"Y'all can be special"

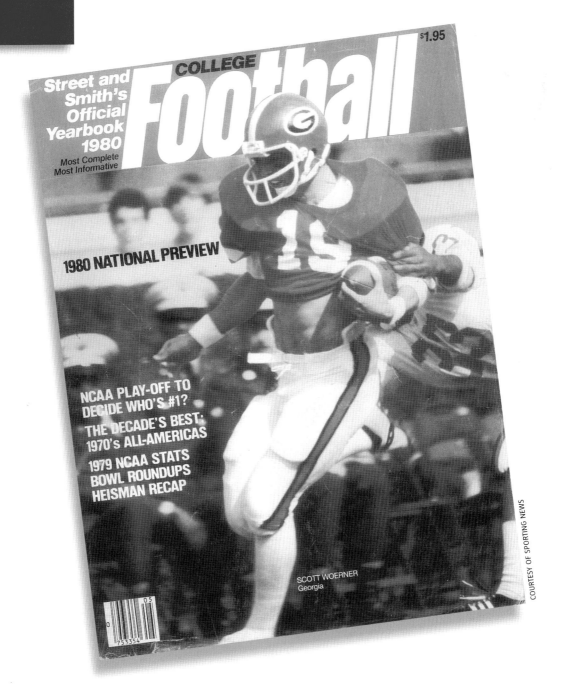

The 1979 season was a disappointment for the Georgia Bulldogs and a disaster for the Florida Gators. The previous nine seasons with Doug Dickey at the Gator helm were marked by inconsistency, unfulfilled potential and broken dreams of a first SEC crown thanks in part to Dooley's Dogs.

Florida had entered the 1975 and 1976 contests as prohibited favorites to depart the Gator Bowl in the SEC driver's seat. Unfortunately for the Gators, they never made it to the steering wheel. Ranked 10th in the Associated Press poll with a 7-1 overall mark and undefeated in the Southeastern Conference (4-0), the 1975 Gators possessed an overpowering wishbone attack with the likes of quarterback Don Gaffney, and the SEC's leading rusher, Jimmy Dubose.

But, Georgia defensive coordinator Erk Russell and his overmatched "Junkyard Dawgs" proved to be the immovable force that countered the irresistible object. Down 7-3 late in the fourth quarter, Georgia's conservative-minded Vince Dooley was forced to throw downfield but not as everyone expected. Out of nowhere, Georgia ran an end around pass and Richard Appleby hit Gene Washington for an improbable 80-yard touchdown that sealed the upset win, 10-7. Alabama would claim yet another SEC title, and Florida would finish second again with Ole Miss and .... the Georgia Bulldogs.

The following year, it looked as if Florida would roll to its first SEC crown. The Gators dominated Georgia and owned a commanding 27-13 advantage at the half. Still leading by seven in the third quarter, Dickey made a call that befuddled everyone in the Gator Bowl and opened the door to a Bulldog stampede. At his own 29, the Florida head coach went for it on fourth and one. No matter the official name of

the play, it will forever be known as "Fourth and dumb." Georgia safety Johnny Henderson and a host of other Junkyard Dogs devoured Florida's Earl Carr for a big loss.

Though Florida still led, the game and the Gators' shot at a first SEC title were effectively over. Six plays later Georgia scored to tie the game and it proceeded to add two more touchdowns for a 41-27 victory. The Bulldogs beat Auburn to secure the SEC championship a week later while Florida fell all the way to third in the final conference standings.

Before the 1979 campaign, Florida raided Clemson's Death Valley and brought the much heralded Charley Pell to Gainesville as its new head coach. Things could not have started worse for the Bear Bryant disciple. The Gators lost five games by 10 points or less and suffered their first winless season since 1946 with a 0-10-1 mark.

Street and Smith's (S&S) 1980 Official College Football Yearbook picked the Gators to finish ninth in the SEC, just above Vanderbilt. They stated that "Things can only get better for Charley Pell and his Gators. Only a scoreless season could be worse than 1979." S&S said "Morale, but not depth, is at a new high with 18 starters back, including ten on offense." Under the tutelage of young offensive coordinator Mike Shanahan, Florida would also install "a pro-style passing game" to resuscitate an offense that finished last in the SEC and near the bottom of the NCAA the year before. Though the pundits were not giving Florida much consideration, and probably with good reason based on its 1979 showing, Pell had a stable of athletes and was laying the foundation for a rejuvenation of Florida Gator football.

After the Wonderdogs thrilled Georgia fans with scintillating finishes in 1978, Georgia entered the 1979 campaign nationally ranked. However, the Bulldogs

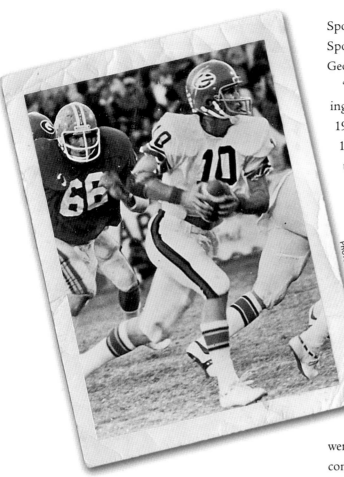

Ray Goff accounted for 30 of Georgia's 41 points in the 1976 comeback win.

Sports Illustrated (14th), AP (16th) and UPI (20th). Sports Illustrated even went as far to explain how Georgia might spend the New Year on the Bayou:

"In the Southeastern Conference's system of rotating opponents, Georgia hasn't played Alabama since 1977 and won't face the Crimson Tide again until 1984. In case of a championship tie, the SEC slot in the Sugar Bowl is denied the team that played there more recently. Thus, if Georgia can tie Alabama for the title this year, it will be the Bulldogs who spend New Year's Day in New Orleans."

S&S chose Georgia to finish second in the SEC but the Bulldogs did not make their pre-season national top 15 list. The national publication did have a hunch Dooley's 17th kennel of Bulldogs might find the bone they had been digging for.

"If the third time is truly a charm, Georgia should go to the Sugar Bowl this year," Street and Smith's wrote. "After all, the Bulldogs, playing as though they were charmed—and sometimes cursed—couldn't have come much closer the last two seasons."

Still, the always conservative Dooley was apprehensive toward the coming season. He was concerned about virtually every position:

- *Offensive line*: "We have no one with the natural blocking ability of a Ray Donaldson. And we only have four players with any experience...but we do have a bunch of fighters — 'Ground Dogs' if you will."

- *Quarterback*: "Buck Belue is the only quarterback with any varsity playing time and he will be coming off a broken ankle suffered in last year's Auburn game. So we have a question mark here."

- *Fullback*: "We lacked production there last year especially due to the injury problem which sidelined

dropped their first three games to Wake Forest, Clemson and South Carolina by a total of 13 points. Georgia bounced back winning five straight Southeastern Conference games, including a 33-10 thrashing of Florida, but lost the SEC finale to Auburn, 33-13, and a bid to the Sugar Bowl. Even a season-ending victory over arch-rival Georgia Tech could not remove the dark cloud of a 6-5 record.

Entering the 1980 season, Georgia was picked by many to be one of nation's top 20 teams. Playboy Magazine chose the Bulldogs sixth followed by

Ronnie Stewart most of the year and Jimmy Womack for several games. With those two...we hope to have more stability. But our fullbacks are still small and have to be at their best to play well."

• *Defensive End*: "Aside from returning starter Pat McShea, we have virtually no experience. Robert Miles has converted from tight end to defensive end in the spring and was a big surprise."

• *Linebacker*: "What we have at linebacker is a bunch of old 'Junkyard Dogs' who have a distinct lack of mobility. They are heavy hitters and are smart but lack the necessary speed for the position."

The key that would ultimately unlock the door to a successful 1980 season was the same component that provided so much heartburn for Dooley the year before.

• *Tailback*: "Tailback is a big question mark. No one really stepped out of the pack last year and established himself and this year's situation is totally wide open. Donnie McMickens had a great spring and Matt Simon and Carnie Norris will also be competing along with Steve Kelly."

MEMORIES

Frank Ros, Georgia linebacker

"You have to take a step back to 1977 when we were the freshman class. That was Coach Dooley's only losing season his whole career. After the 1976 championship, we were supposed to have another good team and it didn't perform to expectations. That was Coach Dooley's only losing season his whole career. That '77 season was something we didn't want to experience again. In 1978, we learned what you can do with good senior leadership and 1979 was the first time Coach Dooley had ever lost three games in a row.

"To me, every experience is a building block. Most of us had experienced the long road to stardom. Only five of us actually dressed and played with the varsity as freshmen. Most of us had gone through scout team, a brutal and humbling experience, and played freshman ball. It wasn't like we had come in and seen instant success. Almost everybody on that team had to earn their right to start. When you do that, it's hard to take a job away from a guy who has worked that hard. I think what you had was a mature group of seniors."

Jeff Harper, Georgia left tackle

"A lot of people say 1980 was just a bunch of guys who came together as a team. It was a little bit more than that. The thing about that team, especially the offensive line, we had played together for a while. There were four seniors starting on the offensive line. We had the mentality that we weren't going to quit.

Jeff Harper

"There was a lot of talent on that team. Everybody had an opportunity to go on and play at a different level. If it wasn't the USFL, it was the NFL. (Tim) Morrison was drafted by the Cowboys and didn't make it. I made it with the Saints. Joe Happe ended up playing and Buck played in the USFL in Jacksonville. Lindsay Scott was a number one to the Saints and obviously Herschel's career.

"When we started practice that August, it was tough. Practice that whole year was difficult. We were out there on that artificial turf and Coach (Wayne) McDuffie was being Coach McDuffie, as hard-nosed as he could be on us. He stayed on us and Coach

(John) Kasay loved on us. Coach McDuffie was just beating us and beating us and beating us from a mental standpoint, but we came out on the other side together. The games were definitely hard, but he had us prepared.

"That team never looked ahead. Everything was focused. We had a goal. They weren't individual goals; they were team goals and nobody cared about who got the glory. We focused on winning one game at a time and controlling our destiny. Once we started climbing, we realized what Coach Kasay would always tell us, 'Y'all can be special. Y'all can be special.'"

"The spring before, we had a sports psychologist talk to the team and he asked, 'What are your goals?' Is it an SEC championship, national championship? Everybody said national championship. He handed out a 3x5 card and said, when's the national championship determined? We said, January 1, 1981. He said, 'Where?' We said, 'In New Orleans.' He said, 'I want you to write down national champions, 'January 1, 1981,' New Orleans. I want you to tape this to your mirror. It will be the first thing you see in the morning and the last thing you see before you go to bed.' I still have that card."

—Frank Ros, Georgia linebacker

3 Georgia's Missing Piece to the Puzzle

In 1979, Georgia possessed talent on the offensive side of the ball. Anchoring the offensive line were All-SEC selections Matt Braswell and Ray Donaldson, also a second and third team All-American selection by the Newspaper Enterprise Association (NEA) and Associated Press (AP). The skill positions returned quarterbacks Buck Belue and Jeff Pyburn, wide receivers Lindsay Scott and Amp Arnold, and tight ends Norris Brown and James Brown.

Still, the Bulldog offense lacked its usual bite, ranking a dismal ninth in the Southeastern Conference in total offense and eighth in rushing offense. Due to injuries, Georgia was forced to impose a tailback by committee strategy with five players carrying the pigskin.

Matt Simon, who missed the first two games against Wake Forest and Clemson with an ankle injury, led the team in rushing with 589 yards, and hardnosed Steve Kelly produced a team leading 5.6 yards per carry. But, there was no one similar to previous tailbacks like Willie McClendon and Kevin McLee who could shoulder most of the load.

On average, opponents out-rushed the Bulldogs 200.5 - 197.9 yards per game. The five times Georgia did not win the ground battle in 1979 resulted in losses. Given the slate of seasoned players returning in 1980, Vince Dooley knew he had to solidify his I-formation for his team to be successful. He quickly figured out his go-to guy.

"In 1980, we had all the pieces to the puzzle, except one," said Georgia team captain Frank Ros, "the big piece right in the middle. We needed a Herschel Walker, a big-time player to carry some of the load. He became that piece."

Walker was the 1979 Parade Magazine "National Back of the Year" from the little town of Wrightsville, Ga. As a senior, he rushed for 3,167 yards and 45 touchdowns leading Johnson County High to the Class A state championship.

"When I saw him in the state championship game, it was like a man among boys," said former Brunswick News sports editor Murray Poole. "Herschel was so big and fast and powerful. They beat a team called Feldwood, and he gained about 350 yards rushing and scored five touchdowns that night. It was surreal for a little stadium to have a Southern California coach and Mike Cavan from Georgia there in the end zone."

Georgia alum Sheila Hoeppner said she remembers her father talking about the high school All-American.

"Dad refereed high school football in Georgia for nearly 25 years and had the pleasure of working both Lindsay Scott and Herschel Walker's high school games," she said. "I remember him telling me before I left to go to school that it was going to be an interesting season because that 'kid from Johnson County was the most amazing runner I had seen in a game.'"

Long-time SEC referee Joe Delany saw it for himself in the season opener against Tennessee in Knoxville where Walker came in as Georgia's third-string tailback.

"I had Herschel in his first game up at Tennessee when he didn't start," he said. "If I remember right, I think a guy named Donnie McMickens started that game. When Herschel came in, a little postage stamp group of Georgia fans stood up and cheered.

"Bobby Gaston asked me, 'What are they cheering about?' I said, 'They just sent that freshman in, Herschel Walker.' He said, 'Which one is Walker?' At the moment, I didn't have enough time to tell him. A few

Tennessee's Bill Bates will never forget his first meeting with Herschel Walker.

plays later, Herschel ran over (Bill) Bates in the end zone. I went up to Bobby and said, 'In case you didn't know it that was Herschel Walker.' He proved to me that day he was not the typical back."

In 1980, Walker rushed for 1,616 yards, 15 TD's and had four games with 200 or more yards rushing. The 1979 team alone gained only 2,177 yards, ran for 13 TD's and rushed for 200 plus yards four times.

He set freshman NCAA marks in rushing, most 200-yard games, average yards per game (146.9), all-purpose yards (1,805), and rushing TDs while earning consensus All-American honors. As the missing piece, Walker was the perfect fit.

"They had one, one superstar," said Frank Tilton, former Savannah Morning News sports editor. "He brought everybody to a bigger height."

MEMORIES:

Claude Felton, Georgia sports information director

"A little background beyond the ballgame, my first year in 1979 we were 6-5 and did not go to a bowl game and didn't have Herschel Walker. That team was essentially the same team that we had in 1979. If you look at those starters, most of that offensive line, Buck and Lindsay, a lot of those defensive guys were there in '79. That team was just missing the Herschel Walker puzzle piece. The addition of him really was the last piece that really made them a great team."

Vince Dooley, former Georgia head football coach/athletic director

"It certainly was a disappointment in '79, but I knew we had a good football team coming back. The missing link to the puzzle, as I've said so many times, was the tailback and that's what Herschel provided. Herschel will tell you today, he was very fortunate when he came. He had a heck of a supporting cast. They were a good football team with a lot of good players that had some great experience. These guys had been around, and they were hungry."

Jeff Harper, Georgia left tackle

"In 1978, if we don't tie Auburn, and in 1979, if we don't lose to them at home, we go to the Sugar Bowl. The '78 team was called The Wonderdogs. The '79 team had a lot of great talent on it but for some reason or another, it didn't come together. We also had Buck (Belue), a lot of good offensive linemen, the same wide receivers and good tight ends. The only thing we really didn't have was Herschel Walker."

Page 7A

The Macon Telegraph

MONDAY MORNING, APRIL 7, 1980

Sports

Harley Bowers

g Heroes.

Walker Signs With Georgia, Ends Long Recruiting War

Tim Groves, Florida safety

"I can remember watching game tapes and saying, 'My Lord.' Herschel Walker could out run you; he could put a little move on, put you on your heels and run right over you. There have been a lot of great ones, but that guy was like Superman. I'm a Florida Gator through and through, but he was the best SEC back ever."

Frank Ros, Georgia linebacker

"In 1980, we had all the pieces to the puzzle except one, the big piece right in the middle. We needed a Herschel Walker, a big-time player to carry some of the big load. He became that piece."

Robin Fisher, Florida nose guard

"Yeah. Yeah. He was the real deal. The best running back I ever played against, by far. It was like hitting a truck."

Freddy Jones, former Georgia beat writer for The Macon Telegraph

"The whole recruiting process, I'd never seen anything like it. I spent nights over there (in Wrightsville). It was Easter Sunday (1980), and I never will forget. I got the call from Herschel's (Johnson County) high school coach, Gary Phillips. He said, 'You better get over here, it's going down.' I'm in Macon and I've got to get to Wrightsville (Georgia). I jump in the car, and I'm probably doing 80-85 mph. I come up the hill outside of Wrightsville, and I get stopped by a Georgia state patrolman.

"He pulls me over, and I said, 'Listen, I know you've heard all kind of stories but Herschel is signing. I've got to get there. I'm working with the newspaper, and I know I'm speeding.' The guy looks at me and says, 'Who is he signing with?' I said, 'He's signing with Georgia.' The guy just pumps his fist, and he says, 'Can I call my boss?' I said, 'Yeah, you can call your boss.' He said, 'You need to get to Wrightsville. Take off and go Dawgs.' No warning. It was big to everybody in the state of Georgia. I never will forget that he wanted to know if it was alright if he called his boss.

"I was the only daily paper there and the hometown paper from Dublin was also there. I was inside with Herschel and his family. If I'm remembering this right, and I'm pretty sure I am, Coach Dooley had used up his visits. So, Coach Dooley had to stay outside while Herschel signed the papers. That's one story I can't get beat on."

4

Polls, Populace and Prognosticators

Uga III

PHOTO COURTESY OF RANDY MILLER

Chaos reigned in college football seven days before Georgia and Florida clashed in Jacksonville. To move further up the national ladder, No. 4 Georgia would need help from some unlikely sources.

Mighty Alabama, owner of the 1978 and 1979 national titles, was still ranked No. 1 with a 7-0 record as it entered Starkville, Miss. Poised to garner another national crown, Bear Bryant's Crimson Tide was shocked by the Mississippi State Bulldogs, 6-3.

It was Alabama's first loss to the Bulldogs since 1957, and Bryant's "Red Elephants" would lose two weeks later to Notre Dame, 7-0, to finish the season with a 10-2 record. The Crimson Tide would not sit atop the throne of college football again until 1992.

Second-ranked UCLA entered its showdown against Arizona with a 6-0 mark. The undefeated record included a 17-0 shutout over then No. 2 Ohio State at The Horseshoe in Columbus, Ohio. The Bruins possessed a high-powered offense that had produced 30 or more points four times.

Coming off a 32-9 thrashing of California, UCLA looked to make a clean sweep of its two-game, PAC-8 road swing, but it was not to be. The Wildcats upset the Bruins 23-17 and sent them tumbling in the national polls to eighth. UCLA lost the next week at home to Oregon and was effectively put out of the running for ita first national championship since 1954.

As its Top 10 counterparts were falling fast, Georgia outlasted No. 14 South Carolina in a physical brawl, 13-10, Between the Hedges in Athens. Nearly an hour-and-a-half after beating the Gamecocks, Dooley released a statement regarding Mississippi State's stunner over Alabama:

"It points up what can happen to any team at any time. After beating Southern Mississippi and Tennessee so convincingly, everyone said Alabama was the 'super' team. But it shows again that you can't look past any opponent. And it says again what I have mentioned for so long and is often referred to about me. That you can't count on beating any team. It emphasizes greatly our game with Florida next week, a team that has already beaten Mississippi State, which upset Alabama."

Georgia entered Jacksonville with its loftiest ranking in nearly four decades, as the No. 2 team in America, and its quest for a first national championship very much alive. The Bulldogs received 11 first-place votes to Notre Dame's 29 in the weekly UPI poll and 15 to the Irish's 47 in the AP. The Nebraska Cornhuskers, 7-1-0, was the only other team in the UPI rankings to have a first-place vote. After manhandling Auburn, 21-10 at Florida Field, the Gators broke into the rankings at No. 20.

THE PREVIOUS WEEK

No. 1 Alabama shocked by Mississippi State, 6-3

No. 2 UCLA lost to Arizona State, 23-17

No. 6 North Carolina lost to Oklahoma, 41-7

No. 11 Baylor was upset by San Jose State

No. 13 Texas lost to Texas Tech

No. 14 South Carolina lost to No. 4 Georgia

No. 15 Missouri lost to higher-ranked Nebraska

No. 19 Arkansas lost to Rice

AP RANKINGS THE WEEK OF GEORGIA-FLORIDA

1. Notre Dame (47)	7-0-0
2. Georgia (15)	8-0-0
3. FSU (1)	8-1-0
4. So. Cal (1)	6-0-1
5. Nebraska	7-1-0
6. Alabama	7-1-0
7. Ohio State (1)	7-1-0
20. Florida	6-1-0

As the college football pollsters elected a new number one team, the American populace went to the election polls on Tuesday, November 4 to decide the next President of the United States. Over 86 million citizens turned out and chose Ronald Reagan over incumbent and Georgia native Jimmy Carter to lead America into the new decade. Jack Hairston of the Ocala Star Banner, though, found this was not the number one thing on the minds of some college football fans. He wrote:

"One fellow remarked Monday, 'Gainesville, Athens and Jacksonville are probably the only towns in America this week that rank the Presidential election and the hostage situation as the No. 2 and No. 3 stories.'

"His companion said, 'Those other things don't really matter. The only thing that matters is whether the Gators can stop Herschel Walker.'

"I wouldn't go that far, but I would wager that I'll be asked more questions about Florida-Georgia this week than Walker Cronkite will be about those other huge matters."

Both the Gators and the Dogs had enormous opportunities set before them. The Lakeland Ledger's Patrick Zier detailed what was at stake for each:

"They are going for the big one at Georgia this year; make that the BIG ONE.

"A national championship. About the only thing that has eluded Vince Dooley down through 17 illustrious seasons he has guided the Bulldog football fortunes.

"And they are also going for the big one at Florida, where the aim is not so high but the incentive is no less great, the big one in this case being Florida's first ever SEC championship, or share of same.

"They cannot both reach their goal, Georgia and Florida. One of them will fall by the way Saturday in Jacksonville, where they renew one of the South's classic rivalries. And historically, most of the time when this game means anything, and it means so much to both this year, Georgia wins it."

MEMORIES

Frank Ros, Georgia linebacker

"Keep in mind, Notre Dame was coming down to play Georgia Tech that week. There wasn't a whole lot of talk that if Georgia Tech beats Notre Dame and Georgia beats Florida, Georgia will be number one. It never entered anybody's mind that Notre Dame was going to either tie or lose to Georgia Tech. We realized even if we beat Florida and Notre Dame beats Georgia Tech, we weren't going to be number one. The funny thing is we didn't allow ourselves to look forward. I don't remember us taking ourselves there. It was a credit to the coaches who kept us focused on one game at a time."

Joe Happe, Georgia center

"As preparation goes, I knew it would be a completely different game for us. The week before against South Carolina, I played against a big, big nose guard called Emanuel Weaver. His nickname was the 'Center Killer,' and he was a big physical guy who tried to blow you up. Robin Fisher was the complete opposite. He was like me, more of a finesse player. I knew I had my work cut out."

Vince Dooley, former Georgia head football coach/athletic director

"For the most part, we just went about our business of preparing ourselves without a great deal of emotional buildup and let the emotions peak at the right time. From that standpoint, I didn't ever feel like that I had to find a way...I was more concerned with playing Vanderbilt or Kentucky than I was with playing Florida."

Wayne Peace, Florida quarterback

"Georgia had such a huge history. I remember watching Buck Belue, Coach Dooley and defensive coordinator Erk Russell on television when I was in high school, and here I was going to be on the same field to play against them."

Leonard's Loser prediction

Florida vs. Georgia

The Red Clay Hounds could be in for a big let down after fighting Chickens all over North Georgia last weekend. And I can assure the Dogs that this ain't no time to ease up when they've got a Crocodile looking down their throat in Jacksonville. Charley Pell's crop of Alligators are big and strong and would like nothing better than to remove the K-9's sweet tooth and ruin a trip to the Sugar Bowl on New Year's Day, but the Bulldogs have a way of upsetting the best laid plan of the Giant Water Lizards each year about this time.

Leonard's Loser - Florida by 10

LEONARD'S LOSERS
COLLEGE and PRO FOOTBALL FORECAST

5

2 Georgia— A National Championship looms

It had been nearly four decades since Georgia had been this close to sitting atop the college football world...even if for a very brief moment.

The last time it happened was 1942 and the United States was fully embroiled in World War II. The fall of that year would be the last opportunity for thousands of young men to play college football. Soon, they would exchange their helmets and shoulder pads for fatigues and M1 rifles, and their dreams of touchdowns and Saturday victories to praying for just one more day to live.

Their battles "in the trenches" on college gridirons around America would be replaced by the hell and horror of war's bullets, bombs, blood and death in the European and Pacific theaters...with many to never return.

The 1942 Bulldogs were led by "Fireball" Frank Sinkwich, who would win the Heisman Trophy that season and accept the award in his Marine Corps Dress Blues. He was joined in the backfield by a freshman, who is still arguably the greatest all-around player in Georgia football history, Charley Trippi.

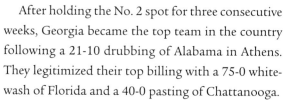

Charley Trippi (left) and Frank Sinkwich (above).

After holding the No. 2 spot for three consecutive weeks, Georgia became the top team in the country following a 21-10 drubbing of Alabama in Athens. They legitimized their top billing with a 75-0 white-wash of Florida and a 40-0 pasting of Chattanooga.

But, November 21, 1942 was the last time a Georgia Bulldog football team held the top spot in the Associated Press (AP) college football poll. Wallace Butts' Bulldogs were upset by the Auburn Tigers 27-13 on the Memorial Stadium turf in Columbus, Ga. They fell from first to fifth and finished the season 11-1 with a 9-0 Rose Bowl win over UCLA and No. 2 AP ranking.

The 1942 squad was crowned national champions by six NCAA recognized polls: DeVold, Houlgate, Litkenhous, Williamson, Poling and Berryman, but AP chose the 9-1 Ohio State Buckeyes, from the Big Ten Conference, instead. Led by legendary coach Paul Brown, Ohio State was also chosen No. 1 by the Boand System, Dunkel System, College Football Researchers Association, and National Championship Foundation. The Helms Athletic Foundation poll picked another Big Ten team, the 8-1-1 Wisconsin Badgers, as its national champions.

Three years later, led by war veteran Trippi, Georgia rolled to a 10-0 undefeated season and a No. 3 ranking in the final AP poll. They were chosen as the nation's top squad by the Williamson Poll but the 8-0-1 mark of Frank Leahy's Notre Dame Fighting Irish was deemed as college football's best by 10 different ranking systems.

Over the next three decades, the Bulldogs appearances in the top five national rankings were rare. Georgia was ranked third one more time on October 9, 1967 and as high as fourth in 1965, 1966, 1968 and 1976 with the final three years resulting in SEC championships via the guidance of Vince Dooley.

During this stretch, other SEC schools like Tennesee (1951), Auburn (1957), LSU (1958), and Alabama (five times) won either the AP or UPI national crowns, and Johnny Vaught's 1959 Ole Miss Rebels were picked as the Football Writers Association of America national champion.

So, entering its November 8, 1980 showdown with the No. 20 Florida Gators, and only one rung away from No. 1, Dooley told the Athens Banner-Herald that his team's focus was paramount.

"We've got to keep our concentration on Florida," he said. "It is great for everybody to think of all the possibilities. But it doesn't help us to prepare to win. I've not thought about anything else but Florida. There is so much to occupy your mind in preparing to win from Florida is a full-time process. There is not time to think of anything else. We are going to think about the positive opportunities we have. Playing Florida is foremost in our minds right now."

Georgia players knew how special the moment was and could be.

"The opportunity we have right now means a great deal," said Georgia defensive guard Eddie "Meat Cleaver" Weaver. "It's an opportunity that doesn't come along a lot for everyday players. Alabama gets a chance a lot, but everybody else doesn't always have a chance. We know where we came from—6-5 (last year). It's kind of hard to forget that. An opportunity comes now. Where we came from makes it that much greater."

Even Charley Pell clearly saw the picture being painted before his young, but talented team.

"It's obvious to us we are a stepping stone for Georgia to reach the national championship,' he said.

The Bulldogs were not oblivious to how quickly their fortunes could change.

"If we loose Saturday, it's all over," Buck Belue said.

"The only poll that counts much is Jan. 2. If we win the last three games, we'll be there when it's over. We are proud to be ranked that high, but it can be taken away."

Georgia's current position had it on the precipice of unfamiliar territory. It had been 1,976 weeks or 13,525 days since it had last been there.

MEMORIES

Tommy Thurson, Georgia linebacker

Tommy Thurson

"The emotions were good because we hadn't lost a game. We were 8-0, everything was positive and I was having the thrill of a lifetime."

Dee Matthews, '57 Georgia alumnus

"At the beginning of that season, I had a little pair of black sandals, and I started wearing those to the games. A lot of times, we would see Erk and Jean Russell after the game. About midway through the season, three or four games in, Coach Russell said to me, 'Dee, are you going to wear those sandals the whole season?' And I said, 'As long as we win.' He said, 'Even in the cold weather?' I said, 'Even in the cold weather.' They were completely worn out after the Notre Dame, Sugar Bowl win. They went to New Orleans with me."

Lindsay Scott, Georgia split end

"Playing for Coach Dooley, we prepared well for everybody. We took it one game at a time and that's what Coach Dooley preached. We were not looking ahead; Coach Dooley drilled that into us. He kept us out of ourselves. We had some success against Florida and expected to beat them, but knew it would take four quarters. We were very aware we could get beat."

Dee Matthews,
'57 Georgia alumnus

"Barbara Dooley and I called each other every Friday morning that year. We started doing that at the beginning of the year. I would call her at 9 a.m. If we were on the road or whatever, I would call her at nine p.m. We said it's bad, in a way, to love something so much. I would tell her, 'I'm just praying, Barbara.' And she would say, 'Dee, I am too. We just have to go one game at a time.' Coach Dooley used to tell Barbara and me that sometimes we would peak too soon.

"One time I said to Barbara, 'It really does bother me that I pray about winning football games.' Barbara said, 'Dee, I talked to my priest about it, and he said it was o.k. for us to do that because God knows what we're thinking all the time anyway.'"

6 "We've got to find a way to win"

Look at most rankings of the best-ever college football national championship teams, and the 1980 Georgia Bulldogs will not be listed near the top. An ESPN.com Page 2 poll did not list Georgia's lone national title team in the top 10, and they did not receive any votes from the pundits or on-line readers.

Even with the fabulous freshman, Herschel Walker, Georgia was not considered a dominating team. The Bulldogs garnered half of their 12 victories by seven points or less with nail-biting affairs against Tennessee (16-15), Clemson (20-16) and South Carolina that could have easily ended in the loss column. They also struggled to get by Ole Miss (28-21) in Athens and bested an average Auburn squad for the SEC title, 31-21.

The Bulldogs did pound the Southwest Conference's Texas A&M Aggies 42-0 and posted 30 or more points against TCU, Vanderbilt, Auburn and Georgia Tech. On the opposite side of the ball, Georgia had a ball-hawking defense. Coming into the Florida game, Erk Russell's final defensive group led the country with 34 forced turnovers.

Though the Bulldogs won every game, in today's vernacular, the 1980 team would have been lacking in "style points."

Whether it was luck, getting the breaks, destiny or being in the right aplace at the right time, its not just enough to have "things" happen, it is what you do with those "things" that determine your ultimate fate. The 1980 national champions were an opportunistic bunch that took advantage of what others gave them and what they themselves created.

Tennessee (Knoxville, Tennessee; Neyland Stadium; September 6, 1980)

Down 15-0 in the third quarter Georgia suddenly came to life before the largest crowd (95,288) to ever see a college football game in the South. Walker made a stunning college debut and Georgia's defense and special teams made key plays that would become mainstays throughout the 1980 campaign.

PHOTO COURTESY OF RANDY MILLER

Herschel Walker's first collegiate touchdown was in Knoxville.

Offense: Walker, Georgia's third-string tailback entering the game, finished with two touchdowns, 84 yards rushing on 24 carries and an impaling of Tennessee safety Bill Bates into the Neyland Stadium artificial turf.

Defense: Big plays would be a common theme for this unit. Their two, vital goal line stands have nearly been forgotten over the past three decades. The first helped keep the game close while the second sealed the comeback win. Late in the fourth quarter with Tennessee only five yards from the Bulldog end zone, Nate Taylor, the Tifton Termite, forced a fumble and defensive end Pat McShea recovered at the one-yard line.

Special Teams: Junior college transfer Joe Happe made his first game in the Red and Black a memorable one. The Pennsylvania native hit Bates on a punt return and created a momentum changing turnover in the third quarter that resulted in a safety.

Clemson (Athens, Ga.; Sanford Stadium; September 20, 1980)

How can a team run five offensive plays for minus two net yards and still lead 14-0 at the end of the first quarter of play? The Atlanta Journal-Constitution's headline might have had the answer: "Woerner, Lady Luck blunt Tigers' charge". The visiting Clemson Tigers did everything but score enough points in a 20-16 loss 'Between the Hedges' as Georgia took opportunism to its zenith in the 1980 season.

Scott Woerner returns a punt 67 yards for TD in the 1980 Clemson game.

COURTESY OF HARGRETT RARE BOOK & MANUSCRIPT LIBRARY/UNIVERSITY OF GEORGIA LIBRARIESIES

Offense: Hardly any to speak of. Georgia totaled only 157 yards on the day (33 in first half) with 121 on the ground via Walker. Clemson ran 90 plays to only 48 for Georgia.

Special Teams: Nearly two minutes into the game, Georgia All-American Scott Woerner broke four tackles and zig-zagged through Clemson defenders with a 67-yard punt return to give Georgia a 7-0 lead.

Defense: As well as the Clemson defense played, the Bulldog defense showed their grit surviving nearly 100 Tiger offensive plays. Woerner stymied an early Clemson drive when he intercepted Homer Jordan in the end zone and sprinted 98 yards to the Tigers' two. It set up a touchdown dive by Buck Belue and gave Georgia a 14-0 first quarter advantage.

South Carolina (Athens, Ga.; Sanford Stadium; November 1, 1980)

The top two running backs in college football, Walker and South Carolina's George Rogers, met before an ABC nationally televised audience in Sanford Stadium. In a brutally physical non-conference tilt, Walker topped Rogers in yards gained, 219-168, and the Bulldogs held on for a 13-10 win between the nationally ranked teams.

Offense: Two words - Herschel Walker. The Georgia offense ran 63 plays with "Hurricane Herschel", as the Atlanta Journal-Constitution's Jesse Outlar described him, toting the pigskin an amazing 43 times against one of the stoutest defenses in the country. Walker's 76-yard TD burst is arguably the most impressive of his collegiate career considering three South Carolina defenders were within inches of him and he left them clutching air.

Defense: Erk Russell's crew had its hands full with Rogers, who would be crowned Heisman Trophy winner at season's end. With the Gamecock's driving late in the final quarter, to either tie or take the lead, the Bulldog defense continued to make big plays in critical situations. Georgia's Dale Carver hit Rogers sending the ball skyward and Chris Welton recovered at the Bulldog 16 to thwart the rally. Georgia added a final interception minutes later to seal the victory.

Special Teams: All-American Rex Robinson was an integral part of Georgia's offensive attack all year long and proved to be the difference with field goals of 57 and 51 yards.

MEMORIES

Joe Happe, Georgia center

"The Tennessee game, my first game, was huge. I went from a couple hundred people watching junior college games to Neyland Stadium. It was overwhelming. Because I had broken my hand, I could not play center, but special teams coach John Kasay had me on punt coverage. I ran down there and hit (Bill) Bates to cause the fumble that created the safety. They had to punt to us and Herschel took over from there."

Lindsay Scott, Georgia split end

"It started from game one. Someone on offense, defense or special teams always seemed to change the nature of each game. It was (Scott) Woerner against Clemson, (Joe) Happe against Tennessee or (Mike) Fisher against Florida.

"That whole season, defensively, we were always able to

Lindsay Scott

"One of the reasons I think the 1980 (Georgia-Florida) game was so close was the week before against South Carolina took a lot out of Georgia. That was a tough, physical game where both teams kind of beat each other up and Georgia needed a late fumble from George Rogers to put that game away."

—Tony Barnhart, CBS Sports

stop people when we had to, to give us a chance to win. Even after the touchdown catch against Florida, they got the ball back with a chance to win, but Fisher intercepted on the next play. The defense did that all year long."

Bobby Pope, former Mercer University athletic director

"You look at that game (Georgia-Florida), and it was one of three Georgia could have easily lost that year. One was the punt return against Clemson, and two, the late fumble by South Carolina's George Rogers. Georgia lived on the edge, but, hey, they got it done and that's all that counted."

Frank Ros, Georgia linebacker

"Everybody realized what the coaches were telling us, that unless you play your absolute best, you can get beat. You'd see it when we watched films on Sunday afternoon. They were usually the plays that determined the outcome. In the Clemson game, you had (Scott) Woerner returning the punt and intercepting that pass. Against Tennessee, Herschel (Walker) did his thing, and the defense stopped them in four-down territory. We broke George Rogers' hand in the South Carolina game and two plays later he comes back in and fumbles.

"You see all those things and you realize the coaches aren't just trying to fill us full of nonsense. They were right. There were plays separating the winners and the losers in each game. As we went into Florida, I felt like the team had the same attitude. We've got to play our absolute best if we're going to win this thing. We're not good enough to win it with a sub par performance."

Vince Dooley, former Georgia head football coach/athletic director

"We had gotten to the point of that season saying 'Somehow, someway, one more time. We've got to find a way to win.' We had been doing that throughout the season. Something would happen. In the South Carolina game, we couldn't stop George Rogers. He was making seven and eight and six and four. Finally, the big fumble came. So something would happen that would enable us to somehow, someway win. So we carried that theme and somehow, someway we carried on."

"It was all fortuitous"
Frank Tilton, former sports editor
Savannah Morning News

"Every game that year with the things that happened, it was all fortuitous. It was meant to be. I did a piece on Pat McShea and he told me, 'I wasn't where I was supposed to be (on the second goal line stand against Tennessee). I was supposed to have been on the other side. Nate hit the guy, the ball came free and there it was for me. If I hadn't been out of position, I would not have gotten that ball.

"When I did get it, I fell on it where it was right in my sternum. My hands were pinned by five or six Tennessee guys who were all in the bottom of the stack. It seemed like it took forever to unravel this pile. I saw this hand coming closer and closer and closer to where it was about to come under me and grab that ball. The only thing I could do was take the face guard of my helmet and punch it down on his hand with all my might. All of a sudden, his hand just shivered and pulled away."

7

20 Florida and 60-Minute Men

Motivation can come in many sizes, especially after a winless season. Charley Pell wanted his Gators to see improvements they could build on. So, before the 1980 season, he implemented a new, vigorous weight and conditioning program, the likes never seen in Gainesville.

"We emphasized weights and conditioning," said Mike Bugar, who coached the defensive line. "Our kids hadn't done that before with the old staff. Coach Pell believed in it, and we had a lot of success with it at Clemson. When I did end up going to Florida in Coach Pell's second year, we installed all that stuff there. We worked the hell out of them. The players were able to grab onto it and believed in it especially when they started having success."

Jacksonville dentist and Florida Gator booster, Dr. Frank Jenkins, provided motivation via the psychological route. He literally gave the Gators something they could hang their victories on in 1980 - t-shirts.

Before their season opening game against California, Jenkins supplied Florida with an orange t-shirt, embolden in blue letters that read: "California - the first step forward." After its 41-13 dismantling of the Golden Bears, NASA astronaut Neil Armstrong might have termed it as "one giant leap." Either way, Florida was dressed for success.

They followed that with a trouncing of Georgia Tech in Atlanta 45-12 ("A team together-Wreck Tech") and a win in its first SEC game against Mississippi State, 21-15 ("Attack the SEC, I'm the winning edge.").

The slogan for game four vs. the visiting Bengal Tigers was "Me and You can beat LSU". That was before starting quarterback Bob Hewko went down with a season-ending knee injury and the Bayou Bengals

bounced the Gators at Florida Field, 24-7.

Against Ole Miss, Florida was encouraged to "Take up the slack and go on the attack." With freshman quarterback Wayne Peace under center it was a scaled back attack but good enough for a 15-3 win and 4-1 record.

At Homecoming, the Florida defense tossed its first shutout of the season against the Louisville Cardinals, 13-0, and took the t-shirt's advice, "Team Pride, play like a winner."

Sitting at 5-1 overall and 2-1 in the SEC, the Gators entertained Auburn on November 1, 1980 and was reminded: "NIRT - November is the real test." The Gators passed it in Florida Orange and Blue colors with a 21-10 victory.

As usual, the real test in November was taken in the classroom known as the Gator Bowl against Georgia. So many times before, all Florida needed was to pass this rigid exam and it would earn at least a share of the SEC crown. The grade had always come back "F". That didn't stand for Florida, either.

Former St. Petersburg Times sports editor Hubert Mizell, said following the previous season, "It was kind of stunning in 1980 when the Gators got off to a 6-1 start. So the Georgia game became a very big deal. Florida seemed in great position to go 7-1." Vince Dooley was not swayed by the dramatic turnaround.

"Florida was not that far off last year," he said. "They had a lot of injuries last year. They changed quarterbacks. They changed offenses. It was one of those years where nothing fit. Now all of a sudden, they are staying healthy, patching up areas and winning."

Dooley knew what his No. 2 team was in for.

"That front seven, on defense, is the best we've seen - certainly the quickest," he said. "They've made all the right decisions this year. They've been able to handle the adversity of losing the starting quarterback (Bob Hewko). They've brought the young quarterback (Peace) along slowly, and they are, right now, a very good team."

MEMORIES

Robin Fisher, Florida nose guard

"I remember that (slogan on the t-shirt). I remember that. We played 58 1/2."

Wayne Peace, Florida quarterback

"My freshman year, Coach Pell would give us a t-shirt the Friday night before the game. It was always an orange t-shirt with blue lettering on it. It always had a slogan and he would try to tie the game to the slogan. That Georgia game, the t-shirt was, "I'm a 60 minute man." His talk to us was you've gotta play hard for a full 60 minutes. What's interesting about that, it's third down, long yardage, 96 yards to go. It was ironic that was our slogan."

> **The Gators were only 60 minutes away from its own improbable worst to first saga and a major jump in the national polls. On November 8, 1980, they wore another slogan on their chests, near their soon-to-be broken hearts, that read "I'm a 60 minute man."**

Mike Bugar, Florida defensive line coach, 1980-1982

"We had some good players. David Galloway, Robin Fisher, Dock Luckie, Mike Clark. They all ended up playing professionally. Dock was just an amazing athlete for a kid that size. In all these years, I've only been around a couple of guys with that kind of size and that kind of athletic ability. I saw him bench 600 pounds. That was an anomaly then and it's still an anomaly now."

Dock Luckie, Florida defensive tackle

"This is one of the games that meant a whole lot to me. We were really focused. We knew what we had to do and what we had to accomplish."

Jimmy Womack, Georgia fullback

"Florida was most definitely a more physically talented team than us. They had one of the better defenses in the league that year with two of the best linebackers in the country with (Fernando) Jackson and (David) Little. He was a monster. Dock Luckie was one of the best defensive tackles in the country and he could bench 500-

Jimmy Womack

600 pounds easily. There are only two other players I know who had done that, Eddie Weaver, and my brother, Ron Simmons."

Jeremy Foley, Florida athletic director

"When we hired Coach Pell, it was with the expectation that he would get the Gators in the hunt to win that first ever SEC championship. After a difficult first year, here we are in year two, right in the mix. The excitement was high."

8

"So much riding on this one"

(Left to right) Ann Kelly, Gena Farr and Deidre Cummins.

Any Georgia-Florida clash is special, but the 59th meeting between the arch-rivals had movie-like story lines attached to it.

- No. 20 Florida, winless in 1979, and picked by most prognosticators to finish near the bottom of the SEC, was vying to complete a worst to first journey and grab a share of its first conference title in school history.

- Georgia, coming off a disappointing 6-5 season in 1979, was undefeated, ranked No. 2 and in search of its first-ever AP/UPI national championship.

- Entering their biggest game in years, the Gators field general was a green-horn freshman, Wayne Peace, who took over for injured senior signal caller Bob Hewko in a game five loss vs. LSU.

- Georgia was also led by a big freshman tailback from little Wrightsville, Ga. Herschel Walker, the unassuming, 220-pound pigskin carrying poet, had taken the country by storm, and his performance on national television against South Carolina a week earlier solidified his candidacy as a true Heisman Trophy contender.

So, it was appropriate one of the teams went "Hollywood." With fans in the Orange and Blue sections of the Gator Bowl going wild in anticipation, Florida grouped in its tunnel and was led onto the field by a 400 lb mechanical alligator from the motion picture, *Alligator*, which debuted that year.

This sci-fi flick centered on a baby alligator, bought by a young girl, that was abruptly flushed down a toilet by her father. The alligator survived in the sewers under Chicago, fed off of laboratory animal corpses that had undergone experimental testing and grew into a behemoth wreaking vengeance upon many unassuming victims.

The message on its movie poster read: "It lives 50 feet beneath the city. It's 36 feet long. It weighs 2,000 pounds. ...And it's about to break out!" That sounded similar to the Florida football program.

From 1973-1976, the Gators won seven or more games each year including nine in 1975 and eight in 1976. Florida was ranked in the Top 10 during the 1975 and 1976 campaigns and went to bowl games each year during that stretch.

After 1976, the Gators slid quickly from an SEC contender to the SEC basement. Over the next three seasons, Florida would win only 10 games overall and go 3-12 in the SEC. Though they went winless in 1979, losing four games by a touchdown or less, Charley Pell's Gators had grown, owned a 6-1 record, and become dangerous again. They were ready to

The Florida team was led onto the field by a 400 lb mechanical alligator.

PHOTO COURTESY OF WILLIAM WINBURN

"break out" for at least a share of their first SEC title against the hated Bulldogs.

"One of the things that always comes to my mind was walking out of the tunnel at Jacksonville," Florida quarterback Wayne Peace remembered. "I'm 18 years old and I remember the excitement was so huge. I was so pumped, nervous, scared or whatever you want to say. I'm a Christian and my prayer was once this game starts, let me relax and play the game.

"When I walked out of that tunnel, I felt very relaxed, calm, ready to play, and I couldn't hear anything. What I mean by that was there was all this commotion going on around me. I could see the players jumping and getting ready for the game. I remember looking up in the stands; I could see all the people's faces moving, but I literally could not hear anything. It was like this deafening quiet. That's the only way I can explain it, honestly. I remember that point very vividly. It's hard to explain, but as I talk to you about it, I can almost feel it."

Twelve months before, very few felt it. Even though Georgia was still in the running for the SEC title with a 5-5 record, most were there for the atmosphere that is Georgia-Florida, which speaks to the uniqueness of the rivalry. You could not have talked many national sportswriters into coming to Jacksonville to watch two teams play with five wins between them. On this sun-splashed November day in 1980, the Gator Bowl press box was overflowing its capacity.

In his game program column, "Gator Talk", then Florida sports information director Norm Carlson wrote: "At last count, there were 117 writers representing 47 media outlets from Miami to New York City (New York Daily News has two writers here today). In addition, 119 photographers representing 44 media outlets will fill the photo deck and sideline photo areas to absolute capacity."

The day after the game, the Ocala Star-Banner reported 171 sportswriters filled the 131 seat Gator Bowl press box while all the sideline passes available were issued. Representatives from the Orange, Cotton, Sugar, Gator, Tangerine, Liberty and Peach Bowls were also in attendance.

Live television was also in attendance as ABC covered the contest for the 11th time. Network producer Terry O'Neil said "65 percent of the country" would see the Top 20, regional clash.

"There are other regional games in this time slot, but Georgia-Florida is going to all the Northeast, Mid-Atlantic, Southeast and Pacific," he said. "The two outside corridors of the United States are covered. Yes, it's a regional game, but a big region."

The excitement had one sports reporter, Georgia alumnus Tony Barnhart, in a quandary.

"They (Greensboro News & Record, Greensboro, N.C.) sent me to Tallahassee, Florida to cover the game between North Carolina A&T and Florida A&M," he said. "The game was at night. There was part of me that really wanted to get in my car and go down I-10 and talk my way into the Gator Bowl to see the game, but I thought better of it."

The scenarios in play for a next step toward the SEC championship were numerous. The only schools left with undefeated conference records were Georgia and LSU, both 4-0. Alabama was joined by Mississippi State and Florida with 3-1 marks. While the Bulldogs and Gators tangled, LSU welcomed Alabama into Death Valley. The next week, both would be on the road—Georgia at Auburn and LSU in Starkville against Mississippi State.

Each team in question had to knock over certain dominos themselves or have them fall in the right order to wake up in New Orleans on New Years Day.

• If both finished 6-0 or 5-1, LSU would have gone to the Sugar Bowl based on the last-appearance rule.

• If Georgia, Alabama and LSU all finished 5-1, LSU would go to the Sugar. If Georgia and Alabama finished 5-1, the Dogs would get the nod.

• If Georgia, Florida and LSU tied at 5-1, Georgia would be 0-1 in head-to-head competition, Florida 1-1, and LSU 1-0. LSU would therefore go to the Sugar Bowl.

• If Georgia, Alabama and Mississippi State tied, the Bulldogs from Starkville would be 1-0 head-to-head, Alabama 0-1 and Georgia 0-0. Georgia could not be reviewed in head-to-head competition so the last appearance rule would be used to break the tie between Georgia and MSU. MSU would have represented the SEC in the Sugar Bowl because Georgia had played there most recently, 1977 vs. eventual national champion, Pittsburgh.

Before kickoff, legendary Georgia broadcaster Larry Munson spoke to the importance of this particular Georgia-Florida game.

"So much riding on this one," he said. "Time and again now these teams have come into this game, which turned out to be, I supposed, in the last 15 years in particular, an unpredictable thing. One of them has come in reaching for a piece of a title and certainly one of them has always come in here looking at a bowl bid. And, now, today, you've got'em both doing it."

They certainly played like everything was on the line and produced an unscripted masterpiece featuring twists, turns, dejection and elation never before seen or felt in this classic rivalry.

MEMORIES

Barbara Dooley, wife of former Georgia head football coach Vince Dooley

"Back when Vince was the head coach, he never believed in women traveling with the team. It was an old Marine Corps, they were going to battle and didn't need a woman thing. I had to get there on my own, as did all the other coach's wives. We normally would take a commercial flight on Friday or early Saturday morning to get there."

Frank Tilton, former sports editor Savannah Morning News

"The big element was Herschel Walker. The hoopla surrounding Herschel combined with that undefeated record made this game probably bigger than most in modern time."

Robin Fisher, Florida nose guard

"We felt like if we could stop Herschel, we could win that ballgame. We knew he was 60-65% of their offense at that time. We knew he was going to get his yards. Our assignment was to stay between him and the end zone. I think coach Dwight Adams said, 'We know he's gonna get in the kitchen, we just gotta keep him out of the ice box.' That was our goal. We might bend, but don't break. He got his yards but we didn't break till that last play. That was a weird scenario."

GEORGIA STARTING LINEUPS

Offense

QB, 8, Buck Belue (Jr.)
TB, 34, Herschel Walker (Fr.)
FB, 25, Jimmy Womack (Sr.)
FL, 82, Amp Arnold (Sr.)
SE, 24, Lindsay Scott (Jr.)
LT, 66, Jeff Harper (Sr.)
LG, 77, Jim Blakewood (Jr.)
C, 56, Joe Happe (So.)
RG, 76, Tim Morrison (Sr.)
RT, 65, Nat Hudson (Sr.)
TE, 88, Norris Brown (So.)

Defense

LE, 83, Robert Miles (Sr.)
LT, 87, Jimmy Payne (So.)
LG, 61, Eddie Weaver (Jr.)
RG, 94, Joe Creamons (Jr.)
RE, 41, Pat McShea (Sr.)
LB, 47, Nate Taylor (So.)
LB, 48, Frank Ros (Sr.)
CB, 19, Scott Woerner (Sr.)
CB, 31, Mike Fisher (Sr.)
SS, 49, Jeff Hipp (Sr.)
FS, 10, Chris Welton (Sr.)

FLORIDA STARTING LINEUPS

Offense

QB, 15, Wayne Peace (Fr.)
TB, 32, Doug Kellom, (So.)
FB, 30, James Jones (So.)
FL, 21, Cris Collinsworth (Sr.)
SE, 89, Spencer Jackson (So.)
LT, 69, Dan Fike (So.)
LG, 65, Dan Plonk (So.)
C, 77, John Redmond (So.)
RG, 75, Jim Subers (Sr.)
RT, 70, Joe Wickline (Sr.)
TE, 80, Chris Faulkner (So.)

Defense

LE, 57, Tim Golden (Sr.)
LT, 85, David Galloway (Jr.)
NG, 66, Robin Fisher (Jr.)
RT, 72, Dock Luckie (Sr.)
RE, 67, Val Brown (So.)
LB, 51, David Little (Fr.)
LB, 49, Fernando Jackson (So.)
CB, 47, Bruce Vaughan (So.)
CB, 43, Sonny Gillam (So.)
SS, 24, Kyle Knight (So.)
FS, 20, Tim Groves (Sr.)

Officials

Referee: Joe Hicks
Umpire: Pete T. Williams
Linesman: Robert "Bobby" Gaston
Line Judge: Ronnie Baynes
Field Judge: Joe Delany
Back Judge: Ted Thomas
Clock: John Wilson

9 "There goes Herschel"

Even though they were separated by 18 spots in the polls, No. 2 Georgia and No. 20 Florida were evenly matched on paper.

	UGA	UF
First downs	128	129
Time/Poss.	236.41	243.19
Off. Plays	550	567
Turnovers	13	13

It was no different on the defensive side of the ball. Georgia had intercepted 19 passes, was giving up just 139 yards rushing and 8.1 points per game. The Gators had allowed only one touchdown in their previous three games and eight the entire season (three coming in a 24-7 loss to LSU).

Even the head-to-head coaching match-up was close. Charley Pell was 1-2 against Dooley coached teams all-time. His 1977 Clemson team won 7-6 in Athens but lost the following year, 12-0. In 1979, Georgia thumped his first Gators squad, 33-10.

What was shown on paper, played out on the field.

Georgia won the toss and opened with fireworks. On the fourth play from scrimmage, Walker proved why he was the talk of college football. He picked up where he left off the week prior against South Carolina.

The most dangerous player on the field took a pitch from Buck Belue, swept right, stiff-armed Florida free safety Tim Groves and used split end Lindsay Scott's downfield block to complete a 72-yard touchdown run that electrified an already keyed-up crowd.

For the second straight week, the freshman sensation had broken a touchdown run for 70-plus yards. If he wasn't the real deal after the South Carolina game, Walker was with less than two minutes off the Gator Bowl Stadium clock.

Georgia's senior place kicker Rex Robinson added his 91st consecutive extra point to make the score, 7-0.

Bulldog wide receiver coach Charlie Whittemore still gives a lot of credit to the blocks downfield that opened it all up for Walker.

"If you look at the first TD run, you are going to see Norris Brown blocking their defensive end, Amp Arnold made a terrific block on the corner and once Herschel gets down there, Lindsay Scott makes a great block for Herschel to score," he remembered. "We kept that clip in our archives to show people how a play should be executed."

Florida's start could not have been worse as disaster struck on its second offensive play. Freshman quarterback Wayne Peace threw a perfect pass to sophomore split end Spencer Jackson who could not handle it. The deflection was gathered in by Georgia senior cornerback and Jacksonville native, Mike Fisher at the Florida 41.

MISSED OPPORTUNITY #1

It could have been horrific for Florida, but unlike it had in previous games, Georgia did not take advantage of the miscue. It began a theme of missed opportunities that plagued the Bulldogs from taking control of the game early.

Four plays later, at the Florida 36, Belue threw a little behind Arnold who made the catch but was hit by the Gator's Bruce Vaughan as he turned back inside. The ball dislodged and Kyle Knight recovered at his own 21 ending a golden chance for Georgia to go up by two scores.

Both defenses quickly demonstrated why they were the two-best ball-hawking squads in the nation

> "Dogs on the 27 1/2," called legendary Georgia broadcaster Larry Munson. "Amp Arnold breaks out to the right, Lindsay Scott to the left and Joe Happe walks up over the ball. And Florida comes up into a six-two now. Buck Belue looking at it, he's going to pitch it to Herschel Walker, try and get him outside. He's gonna get five, he's got 10, 15, 20, 25, 30, 35, 40. He needs a block. There goes Herschel. There goes Herschel."

with Georgia leading with 35 takeaways and Florida second with 28.

The young Gators did what Georgia could not do, capitalize on the mistake. Florida marched to the Georgia 23 on the strength of Peace's 15-yard pass to Curt Garrett and a 22-yard strike to former quarterback now turned wide receiver, Tyrone Young. The drive stalled there, but place kicker Brian Clark knuckle-balled a 40-yard field goal try just inside the upright to make it 7-3.

It was the first points Georgia had given up in the opening quarter all year (51-3) and helped swing the momentum to the Orange and Blue.

MEMORIES

Wayne Peace, Florida quarterback

"Obviously Herschel Walker had gotten a lot of publicity, and I was looking forward to watching him. Early in the game he hit about a 50 or 60 yarder, and I remember thinking, 'Oh crap, we might have bitten off a little more than we can chew.'"

Joe Happe, Georgia center

"We started out the game with a toss to Herschel and he went all the way. It was really euphoric. We felt, 'O.k., we're going to blow these guys out.' When you score that quick and early, you really need to keep the pressure on. We were unable to do that."

Robin Fisher, Florida nose guard

"There's a picture that day of me on Sports Illustrated diving at Herschel's feet. I can remember taking off and running down the line trying to beat him outside. I tripped over our linebacker, Fernando Jackson, just reached and I was on the cover of Sports Illustrated. I still have a copy of it somewhere."

10 Meanwhile, back in Atlanta...

GEORGIA TECH
VS.
NOTRE DAME
November 8, 1980
Grant Field/$1.50

Five hours north of Jacksonville, the supposed beat-down was to commence at 1:30 p.m. on Grant Field's artificial turf. The beleaguered Georgia Tech Yellow Jackets, winners one time in eight games, were hosting the undefeated, top-ranked team in America, the Notre Dame Fighting Irish.

Tech was coming off a loss the week before that brought this headline from the Atlanta Journal-Constitution (AJC): "Tech hits a new low in 17-12 fall to Duke." The Yellow Jackets lone victory for its first-year head coach, Bill Curry, had come against Memphis, 17-8.

Notre Dame was 7-0, and had scored 25 or more points six times. On the flip side, Tech had given up 192 points and scored only 82. The Irish were averaging 286 yards on the ground and yielding only 97. The AJC said, "Tech will have extreme difficulty moving the football." Neither the recitation of Hail Mary's, rubbing of Rosaries, nor the lighting of prayer candles appeared it would help the outmanned Yellow Jackets in this gridiron mismatch.

The AJC analyzed it this way: "What else does Tech need? It has had three bad years of recruiting, creating a vast talent shortage, and one season of injuires, further depleting that shortage. Now, it must play the No. 1 team in America with No. 2 Georgia waiting three weeks down the schedule." For many fans and football aficionados, the AJC's prediction was down-right kind, "Notre Dame by 38." The official line favored the Irish by 20.

AJC columnist Jesse Outlar proclaimed: "In Atlanta, Notre Dame, the No. 1 team, visits Georgia Tech. Even if the Irish are looking ahead to next Saturday's 'bowl' against Alabama in Birmingham, it's bound to be a rout, say Notre Dame 44, Georgia Tech 10."

With the major upsets of No.1 Alabama and No. 2 UCLA a week earlier, Notre Dame head coach Dan Devine was not looking to the horizon where Alabama waited for the Irish on November 15. The veteran coach had experienced the same situation 20 years earlier.

"I don't really put that much faith in the polls," he said. "I made that mistake once in 1960. Our Missouri team beat Oklahoma badly (41-19) in Norman in the next-to-last game of the season, and we jumped to No. 1. We stayed there one week. The next week we lost to Kansas.

"Frankly, all I'm thinking about is Georgia Tech, not being No. 1 or having to face Alabama or Air Force or USC. Ask me about being No. 1 and the national championship after New Year's Day."

Curry, who was on staff that last time Georgia Tech beat the Irish in 1976, knew the gravity of the challenge his charges would face.

"We've got to be aggressive. If you're going to make a mistake, make an aggressive mistake because if you play it the other way and tighten up, they'll kill you. A team like them will just blow you away."

The "Run and Shoot"

Little did the nearly 69,000 people in the stands and millions watching the annual clash on ABC-TVs regional telecast know they were witnessing a precursor to how college football, especially in the SEC, would evolve. In a conference that for so long had been predicated on the ground game, Florida's young offensive coordinator, Mike Shanahan, introduced them to an air attack called the "Run and Shoot."

"At that time, the SEC was still more of a pound it out, play action style offense," Shanahan reflected. "In 1979, when I was at Minnesota, it really worked in the Big Ten. I think the only thing that was different at Florida was we always had one tight end tight, and a one back set. That was where we actually had the four wide receiver look. The year before, they (Florida) were in the Power-I, and dead last in offense. We went from one extreme to another."

The offensive principles were originally devised in the 1960s by high school coach Glen "Tiger" Ellison in Columbus, Ohio. The Run and Shoot concept centered on spreading out the defense with four wide receivers, thus, taking away their ability to use its regular blitzing and stunting concepts.

The Run and Shoot was popularized in the collegiate ranks by Portland State's Mouse Davis beginning in 1975. Under his guidance, Portland State would average 49.2 points per game in 1980. It would birth disciples like June Jones, who played quarterback for Davis and used the principles later as a professional and collegiate coach.

With the Minnesota Golden Gophers, Shanahan's offense produced numbers never before seen in school history. They set records that included most passing yards (2,309), passing yards per game (209.9), attempts and completions (317-185), most total yards in a season (4,108), most total yards per game (373.5), most points (264), and most points per game (24).

It turned quarterback Mark Carlson into Minnesota's greatest single season passer ever at that time. He threw for 2,188 yards, 11 TDs and twice threw for over 250 yards. Minnesota quarterbacks had reached the 250-yard mark only five times prior to 1979. Under Shanahan's tutelage, Carlson also led the Big Ten in passing and total offense per game. As a team, Minnesota led the conference in passing offense.

Larry Munson, a Minnesota native, said of the "Run and Gun" as he called it: "I remember how the Minneapolis papers raved about it when they put it in at Minnesota only one year ago."

The Florida offense took to it like Alligators to the Okefenokee Swamp. The Gators opened 3-0 scoring 107 combined points on California (41), Georgia Tech (45), and Mississippi State (21). That topped the total output of 106 points over 11 games from the previous year.

"It's really wide open," Florida wide receiver Spencer Jackson said earlier in the season. "Any one person can get the ball at any time. With a man in motion and several receivers on every pattern, it can really confuse the defense."

Since it couldn't match Georgia physically, Florida aimed to use the Run and Shoot to confuse, and stretch the Bulldogs' formidable Wide Tackle Six defense.

"We were a young, undersized team, playing a young quarterback who probably shouldn't even been playing," Peace said laughing. "Georgia was an extremely strong, physical team. We needed to try and do everything we could to spread the field and try to make it a little easier on us. If they kept everybody close to the line, then we'd throw the ball. If they tried walking people off and covering the receivers, that would help us in the running game."

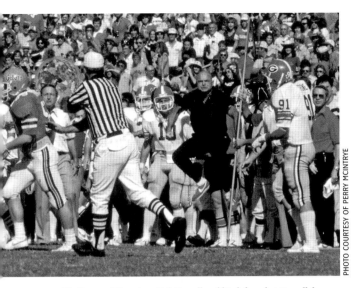

The Run and Shoot kept Erk Russell and his defense hopping all day.

PHOTO COURTESY OF PERRY MCINTRYE

"Of course, their defensive coordinator, Erk Russell, was one of the best and did a great job supporting the run," Shanahan said. "We thought by spreading them out a little bit, we could throw and run the football a little more effectively. We had Jamie (James) Jones as a running back, half-back, full back type of guy. It wasn't like we had a great game offensively, but we had a chance to win it there in the fourth quarter."

Years later, Shanahan learned that the ABC's color commentator, Frank Broyles, had questioned Florida for staying in the set the entire game.

"It was something they had not seen," Shanahan said nearly three decades later. "We stayed in that formation and it worked fairly well for us."

After the game, Russell knew his defense was the one that had been in "trouble."

"I think they did exactly what they had to do to win this game," he commented after the contest. "They couldn't come at us from an 'I' and they knew they had to hit us with a scattered attack. They did

that, all right. I think they picked us better than any team we've played...Florida brought it to us."

And they did it in atypical SEC fashion.

MEMORIES

Mike Shanahan, Florida offensive coordinator, 1980-1983

"I was really proud of Wayne Peace. For a freshman coming in that atmosphere and doing a good job, really managing the game. Giving you a chance to win in the fourth quarter is about all you can ask."

Vince Dooley, former Georgia head football coach/athletic director

"They were ready to play and made it tougher because they spread you out a little more. That would be a credit to the offensive coordinator, Mike Shanahan. He was a very good offensive coach, and he was a little head of the curve. They did some different things we were not prepared for. One of those was getting the ball to that big, tall receiver (Tyrone Young) in the open space. That gave us some fits in the ball game."

Rex Edmondson, Florida Times Union

"It was a case of justifiable homicide as far as Georgia was concerned. They confessed the Gators had befuddled them defensively most of the day with their offensive formation, sort of a variation of the old Double Wing or Double Set or whatever you want to call it."

Frank Ros, Georgia linebacker

"I think it was smart of him to spread us out because we were probably better together than we were separately. We didn't have the greatest athletes. Our defense thrived on bringing it at us. We were strong

Chapter 11   **65**

defensively in that area with (Eddie) Weaver, (Tim) Crowe, myself, and Nate (Taylor) in the middle. It wasn't like we weren't capable of defending against it. We just contributed by being overzealous and not being fundamentally concentrated."

Jeremy Foley, Florida athletic director

"Mike Shanahan was our offensive coordinator, and we did some different things. It obviously had us in a position to win until one of the most amazing plays in the history of college football happened."

Frank Tilton, former sports editor
Savannah Morning News

"After the game, I interviewed Lindsay first, Buck second, Herschel third and Coach Dooley fourth. Very, very hesitantly and reluctantly did I go to the side room where Erk Russell and his assistant coaches were. They were not happy at all. I remarked to him that June Jones had said that offense could not be stopped. Erk pretty much said, 'Baloney. What happened is we didn't tackle. If you watch the game film, you will see most of those passes were short and their receivers broke the tackles and made great yardage.' It was unbelievable that offense had accomplished so much against an Erk Russell defense."

Wayne Peace, Florida quarterback

"I had only started a few games before facing Georgia. We played Ole Miss my first game and hardly threw the ball at all. We played Louisville next, and they had to let me throw the ball a little bit against Auburn. It went very well, and we beat them.

"The only chance we had to compete with Georgia was to open the thing up a little bit. They played a Wide Tackle Six and had excellent players. We didn't feel like we could line up, be physical and overpower them. That's why we went to the four wide receivers and spread the field a little bit to take advantage of our playmakers with Tyrone Young and Cris Collinsworth. All week long at practice, I really struggled with it. I didn't have a good week of preparation at all, and here we were playing the number two team in the country thinking, 'My gosh I just had the worst week of practice I've had in years.' It was not a real good feeling going into that game."

"They will not be able to stop this attack"

Frank Tilton, former sports editor Savannah Morning News

"A couple of weeks before the game, June Jones, who had been involved with the implementation of the Run and Shoot, made an appearance at the Savannah Quarterback Club. I had read a few articles on Mouse Davis at Portland State and his Run and Shoot pupils Mike Shanahan and Jones. It was an exciting offense and the first year it had been implemented at Florida. With the Florida game coming up, I asked June about this offense. He said, 'They (Georgia) will not be able to stop this attack.'

"Two famous defenses being chopped up"

During the first half of the second quarter, the momentum of the game would be tossed back and forth like the ocean waves hitting Jacksonville Beach. In less than eight minutes, Florida and Georgia ran 27 total offensive plays with each scoring a touchdown and committing a turnover.

The second quarter began as the first did, very well for Georgia. On third and 10, Buck Belue ran for nine yards and a late hit by Florida's Robin Fisher took the Bulldogs from the Florida 44 to the Florida 20. Herschel Walker toted the pigskin two consecutive times to give Georgia third and three at the Gators 13.

With a Power I formation of Ronnie Stewart, Jimmy Womack and Walker behind Belue, everyone in the Gator Bowl was looking for Walker to blast his way for a first down and possibly more. Instead, Georgia gave Florida a little of its own medicine. Belue rolled left and floated a pass to Stewart who made a twisting catch that propelled him into the end zone for the 13-yard touchdown reception.

Jimmy Harper congratulates Ronnie Stewart on his TD reception.

"Did you see Stewart turn around and catch that ball," Georgia announcer Larry Munson said after the score. "He turned around and saw it and reached up, turning back to face the passer and went in there with that orange shirt on him."

Freddie Gilbert celebrates Georgia's recovery of a Florida fumble.

Robinson's point-after made it 14-3 and with just over 13 minutes left, the pendulum had swung back to the Red and Black.

Eerily similar to the opening stanza, Florida committed a turnover on the second play of its first drive of the second quarter. Georgia defensive end Jimmy Payne stripped Wayne Peace of the ball and defensive tackle, Eddie "Meat Cleaver" Weaver recovered at the Florida 25.

MISSED OPPORTUNITY #2
The Gators were reeling and dangerously close to the point of no return. Georgia was salivating with a chance to put a vice grip on the game.

On third and four from the Gator 16, Georgia went to the air again. Belue tried to hit Amp Arnold on an out pattern, but Florida cornerback Ivory Curry timed it just right, stepped in front for the interception and returned it 22 yards.

"Yeah, we really regretted that missed opportunity because you could feel that momentum was changing," Joe Happe said. "It was slowing down for us and they were really kicking in with their confidence. You just knew it was going to be a battle."

Of the interception, Munson told his listeners to, "Remember now, she's (Florida) famous for those things just as the Dogs have been."

It was the break Florida needed and allowed the Orange and Blue faithful to breathe new life or maybe just a sigh of relief. Waiting to explode, the Red and Black contingent had their bubble popped again.

Florida did little with the second turnover, but the Bulldogs were not finished with their giving ways. Two plays into Georgia's third possession of the quarter, Walker uncharacteristically fumbled and it was recovered by Sonny Gilliam at the Georgia 46.

With the Run and Shoot, the young Gators wasted no time biting off big chunks of yards.

"I think we made our share of mistakes but clearly," Happe said, "they were a talented team. They kept coming back and showing great character."

Florida began the drive as senior Cris Collinsworth took an end around for 12 yards.

"This is the wide open offense they had earlier in the year as they were eating people alive," Munson moaned. "Then they got conservative when they lost their quarterback early in the LSU game."

James Jones then pounded the Georgia defense for 12 more. After an incompletion, Peace hit Collinsworth, who made a one-handed catch, for 13 that spurred Munson to say, "Two famous defenses being chopped up."

Florida ended the barrage as Peace lofted a perfect nine-yard pass to Collinsworth, just over Georgia's Scott Woerner, for the score. What could have been as much as an 18-point Georgia lead was now trimmed to only a four-point Florida deficit, 14-10.

The last seven minutes saw only Georgia cross midfield and eventually commit its fourth turnover, but more importantly, both teams lost key players to injury. The Bulldogs lost a playmaker in wide receiver Arnold. The senior suffered a knee injury at the end of a 16-yard run by Walker.

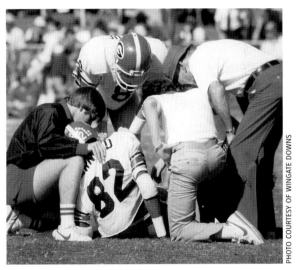

Georgia's offense lost a big weapon when Arnold went down.

"Right leg or knee," Larry Munson said from his perch high above the Gator Bowl. "There goes that tremendous flanker out of Athens being helped off the field. He has hurt his right knee, apparently. That's a bad sign. We lost the starting center for the year. We may, I'm guessing, have lost a flanker now."

Arnold came into the game as Georgia's leading receiver and had already caught a 91-yard touchdown pass against Kentucky two weeks earlier.

"One of the things very few people have talked

about was the impact of losing Amp in our attack," wide receivers coach Charlie Whittemore said. "He was a key player in our offense. Amp made some big plays all through his career. In 1978, he made a great touchdown catch against Tech to come from behind and got the two-point play that helped us win 29-28. He had a 91-yard TD pass against Kentucky earlier in 1980."

The injury would keep Arnold out the remainder of the regular season but the Athens, Ga. native did return two months later in the Sugar Bowl making Georgia's only reception against Notre Dame.

Three plays after Arnold went down, senior Dock Luckie, a key ingredient on Florida's defensive line was lost for the rest of the game. He remembers the play vividly.

"Midway through the game, one of Georgia's offensive linemen did a chop block on my ankle and twisted it pretty bad," he said. "I tried to come back out and go, but I just couldn't. Their goal was to put me out of the game. They knew I was one of the main point guys for defense. During the first and second quarter, I was making a lot of tackles and they came up with a scheme to try and put me out."

Some Bulldog fans in the stands seemed comfortable with the slim four-point lead. Teni Yarborough, features editor for Georgia's school newspaper, The Red and Black, reported:

"At halftime, the Dogs were leading and dreams of a weekend in New Orleans seemed closer. 'I'm making my reservations right after the game,' one Georgia student said. 'You're too late, I called last night and they said the nearest vacancy is 50 miles away,' his friend answered. 'Oh well, it doesn't matter. I'll still be there,' the first student said."

The Bulldogs on the field knew they had squandered chances to put Florida "out" of the game early. They had been in plenty of close games throughout the 1980 season, but this was different. The ranking, a shot at an SEC and potential national title was hanging by a thread.

Florida's young Gators went into the locker room with the momentum, belief and the knowledge it was well within striking distance of a first-ever SEC championship.

MEMORIES

Lindsay Scott, Georgia split end

"I remember we came out early like gangbusters. We had an opportunity to blow that game open, but we got a little conservative. The opportunities were there if we had opened it up."

Larry Munson, Legendary voice of the Georgia Bulldogs

"I'll tell you one thing, that freshman quarterback Florida's got can really throw the ball because we've had such great pressure on him. They (Georgia) better keep the pressure all day if they want to stay alive."

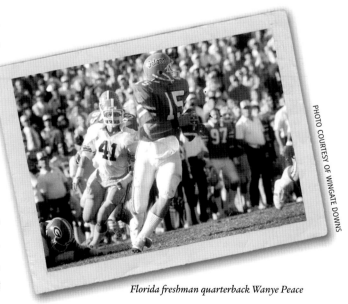

Florida freshman quarterback Wanye Peace

Team Statistics

	Georgia (Visitors)	Florida (Home)
First Downs	9	10
Rushing Yardage (Att/Net Yds)	29-184	18-62
Passing Yardage	50	144
Total Offense	234	206
Return Yardage (Net)	4	22
Passes (Att-Comp-Int)	10-5-2	22-12-1
Punts (Number-Average)	2-41.0	3-33.3
Fumbles-Fumbles Lost	2-2	1-1
Penalties-Yards Penalized	1-5	6-69

> "We've got to have an air arm today for sure because this is too much defense the Gators are sticking out there on us."
>
> — *Larry Munson, Legendary voice of the Georgia Bulldogs*

Individual Leaders

Georgia

Rushing	Att.	Net Yards	TD	Long Run
Herschel Walker	23	149	1	72
Buck Belue	3	28		
Jimmy Womack	2	6		

Passing	Att-Comp-Int	Yards	TD
Buck Belue	10-5-2	50	1

Pass Receiving	No.	Yards	TD
Ronnie Stewart	1	13	1
Lindsay Scott	1	21	
Clarence Kay	1	9	

Punting	No.	Yards
Mark Malkiewicz	2	41.0

Florida

Rushing	Att.	Net Yards	TD	Long Run
James Jones	9	33		
Wayne Peace	6	10		
Cris Collinsworth	1	12		

Passing	Att-Comp-Int	Yards	TD
Wayne Peace	22-12-1	144	1

Pass Receiving	No.	Yards	TD
Spencer Jackson	3	23	
Cris Collinsworth	2	22	1
Tyrone Young	4	69	
James Jones	2	17	

Punting	No.	Yards
Mark Dickert	3	33.3

13

"...maximize the opportunity..."

Georgia had every chance to seize complete control of the game in the third quarter, but the Gators defense would not allow it.

"You want to maximize the opportunity when you have it going," Dooley would say in recalling the game. "We did have it going early. Then, Florida really had the momentum on us and once it turned, they had it at the right time."

Florida received the second half kickoff and was stoned by the Georgia defense. The Bulldog offense started at its own 41 yard line and proceeded to grind the ball in typical Dooley fashion.

Womack took the dive play for four yards. Then Walker carried five straight times for one, six, 15, six and 15 again putting Georgia at the Florida 12. An offside penalty pushed the Bulldogs back to the Florida 17 and the Gator defense stiffened.

MEANWHILE BACK IN ATLANTA…

After backup tailback Carnie Norris gained four to the Florida 13, ABC-TV flashed on the screen that Georgia Tech was leading Notre Dame 3-0 in the second quarter.

With the "major" upsets that occurred the week before, a winless Tech team taking down No. 1 Notre Dame would produce a college football earthquake with powerful tremors extending to the Gator Bowl's 50 yard line.

MISSED OPPORTUNITY #3

On second and 11, Buck Belue rolled left and had Lindsay Scott open in the end zone, but never saw him. Instead, the junior quarterback from Valdosta tucked the ball and ran for five yards. The next play, Belue rolled right and threw to Chuck Jones. Ivory

Curry, who already had one interception on the day, cut in front of Jones and almost corralled his second. Fortunately for Georgia, he could not control it, and the drive stalled there. With 9:38 left in the quarter, Rex Robinson booted a 24-yard field goal to put Georgia up by a touchdown, 17-10.

Wayne Peace and the Florida offense could not generate anything viable on its next possession. They didn't help themselves on the punt either as senior defensive end Rod Brooks committed an unnecessary personal foul that put Georgia in great position at its own 47.

Walker began the drive with a nifty 12 yard gain that gave him 204 yards rushing midway through the third quarter. During the quarter, the fantastic freshman would also establish a new single season Georgia rushing record surpassing Willie McClendon's 1,312 yards in 1978. Jimmy Womack then busted up the middle for seven more and Florida was flagged another 15 yards for a facemask penalty.

Jimmy Womack (#25), an undersized fullback, was a devastating blocker and powerful runner.

The Bulldogs did not let up. Walker swept right for another 13 yards and was tantalizingly close to putting Georgia up by 13 if not for a touchdown saving tackle by Gator safety Tim Groves. With first and goal at the Florida five, Georgia seemed certain to slam the door shut.

MISSED OPPORTUNITY #4

Instead, Walker was slammed by the Florida defense for no gain on first down. The Gators proceeded to stop Georgia's next two attempts forcing Robinson to provide the points. His 20-yarder split the uprights and Georgia extended its lead to 20-10 with 3:58 in the quarter.

In conjunction with providing Georgia a 10-point lead, Robinson's second field goal also gave him 254 career points and tied him as the all-time SEC scoring leader with Charles Alexander of LSU. He would not get another chance to take sole possession of it on this day.

MEANWHILE BACK IN ATLANTA...

In the third stanza, Georgia's defense had limited Florida to 40 total yards of offense while amassing 90 of its own, all on the ground. The Bulldogs had increased its lead by six points and ahead by two scores.

Unbelievably, Georgia Tech was holding firm to its 3-0 lead over Notre Dame at the half. Bulldog fans could only dream that the unthinkable might occur.

Unbeknownst to everyone, unbelievable was sitting nearly 14 minutes away. Before it arrived, Georgia's dreams of an SEC championship and so much more would quickly turn into a Titanic-like descent.

FRESHMAN SEASON RUSHING YARDAGE: Walker compared to recent Heisman winners

Earl Campbell *Texas*	**928** yards
Archie Griffin *Ohio State*	**772** yards
Charles White *Southern Cal*	**744** yards
Billy Sims *Oklahoma*	**95** yards
Herschel Walker *Georgia* (through eight games and three quarters)	**1,317** yards

The Gator defense closes in on Herschel.

14 "Dogs defense worn to a frazzle"

For a team that did little in the previous 15 minutes, Florida went from zero to 60 on the second play of the fourth quarter.

Facing third and five from its own 35, Wayne Peace hit Tyrone Young on a simple, "quick in" that quickly changed the tone and momentum of the game. The lanky sophomore showed the athleticism that prompted Mike Shanahan to move him from quarterback to wide receiver.

Young first broke Frank Ros' tackle and then attempts by Steve Kelly and Jeff Hipp. He was finally brought down by Scott Woerner, at the 11-yard line, who had pursued the play from across the field to end the 54-yard jaunt.

Larry Munson called it this way:

"Peace just dumps it over the line, complete. He breaks a tackle. He got five, there he goes. Tyrone Young breaks another tackle. 35, 30, 25, 20, one man, Scott Woerner got him around the 12. He broke two or three tackles. They just dumped it over the line for 54 yards down to the Georgia 11.

"They dumped it over to that big six foot, six inch giant flanker who caught it and broke a tackle and went 54 yards."

Georgia's team captain still takes the blame for the play.

"It was a quick hitch pattern, and Tyrone Young made a quick move," Ros remembered. "If we do what we're supposed to do...if I break down before I get to him and tackle him instead of trying to decapitate him, that doesn't happen. I was very disappointed in myself because I contributed to making it a difficult game. That was frustrating because I expected excellence on the field."

Frank Ros

Florida wasted no time in capitalizing. On the very next play, James Jones, who would enjoy a 10-year NFL career with the Detroit Lions and Seattle Seahawks, ripped off right guard, broke Eddie Weaver's tackle and spun into the end zone for the touchdown.

The Bulldogs had been burned and at the same time, a fire was lit under all those in Orange and Blue, especially Charley Pell. The Florida coach elected to go for the two-point conversion that would hopefully produce the game winning field goal later.

It was the right choice. The Gators poured more fuel on the fire as Peace hit Young for the conversion to make it a two-point deficit.

"Now its 20-18," Munson said with concern in his voice. "You can see where the momentum has absolutely gone to the other side of the field."

And it stayed there. Florida's defense yielded a 14-yard run to Herschel Walker on the ensuing first down but completely stuffed the Bulldog offense on the next three plays forcing a punt. With 12:05 to play, the Gators had their eyes set on the lead.

Interestingly, on this drive, Shanahan set up the pass with numerous running plays. Peace ran for eight, and Jones gained nine yards on the next two plays. Peace connected with Cris Collinsworth for seven to the Florida 48. After sneaking for a first down and a two-yard gain by Jones, Peace found his favorite target. He hit Young for 19 to the Georgia 30.

To Georgia's credit, the defense that had come up big all year did so again. On third and four, Nate Taylor knocked down Peace's pass forcing the Gators into a field goal situation. Florida's Brian Clark nailed the 40-yard field goal to give the Gators their first lead of the game with 6:52 remaining.

It evoked delirious delight from Florida fans, and a surprising response from the Florida coach's booth.

"An interesting sideline in the 1980 game was our

Florida's Brian Clark nailed the 40-yard field goal to give the Gators their first lead of the game with 6:52 remaining.

encounter with the Florida coaches," said Dick Payne, longtime Georgia radio spotter. "They were right next door to us. Before the game started, they had used some outlets in our booth to hook up some electronic gear in their booth. When they kicked that field goal to go ahead, they stuck their heads in our window and started screaming and hollering, making a fool of themselves and trying to harass us."

As Munson went to a commercial break, he said, "Florida leads 21-20. Dogs' defense worn to a frazzle."

Florida's wasn't. It had just received an energy boost with dreams of an SEC title only six minutes away. The Bulldog offense could do nothing with the fired up Gators. They registered an offside penalty, two-yard loss by Walker and a pair of incomplete passes by Buck Belue.

The Gators received the ball with 5:53 remaining in the game. They moved from their own 31 to the Georgia 40, taking 4:18 off the clock, before the drive stalled.

"There won't be much time left when the Dogs finally get their hands on the ball," Munson said. "There'll be very, very little. And our long passing game has not done well today at all."

After Florida punter Mark Dickert pinned the Bulldogs on their own eight, Georgia's legendary voice then proved to be an unknowing prophet.

"We have stayed unbeaten all year long, but here we are now inside our own eight and only 95 seconds," he said. "You can't drive it. You've gotta have a long run or a long pass or a short pass turned into a long run with it."

Georgia's first and second down plays did not offer much hope of that happening. Belue was first forced from the pocket and scrambled out of bounds for a one yard loss. ABC then placed a graphic on screen depicting Belue's difficult day: six of 14 passing for 52 yards, one TD and two interceptions.

On second down, it didn't get any better. Belue threw on the run to Charles Junior who dropped the ball while going out of bounds. The third-year quarterback threw his hands up in disgust.

Just like a mother, Belue's mom felt her son's frustration and put his feelings ahead of everything else.

"As I think about that play, I think about my mother after second down leaving the stands and taking a walk to the locker room underneath the stands," Belue remembered. "At the time, she just heard the place going bezerk, and she didn't know what had happened. She was coming to the locker room to console her oldest son."

On the other side of the ball, Munson said Florida was ..."smelling a big, fat juicy win here unless something happens."

Gator fan Dorthia Lamberth agreed.

"I didn't think that we would beat you," she said. "Now, we may have a shot at the Bowl (Sugar Bowl), but I'm sorry, y'all had so much more to lose."

MEANWHILE, BACK IN ATLANTA...

In Atlanta, the Yellow Jackets were on the verge of a monumental upset and even more, providing their bitter rival an assist for the ages, one that could possibly lead to a first-ever national championship.

With less than 10 minutes left in the game, beleaguered Georgia Tech was leading the nation's top ranked team, 3-0.

Everything that any Georgia fan or player could hope for was coming together, but the Bulldogs had dug themselves a hole, one that looked too deep to get out of.

MEMORIES

Carl Brantley, Georgia fan

"One of them (Florida fans) stood up and said something to the effect of, 'Well, there goes your ranking. We did it again.' The Georgia fans were so upset they didn't pay any attention to him. Right after they kicked the field goal, he left. He thought they had it in the bag."

15 Left 76

PRELUDE TO THE PLAY

Even after the mighty Casey struck out, Mudville seemed like a joyous place compared to the Red and Black sections of the Gator Bowl.

"On third down, it was gloom and doom in the stands," Carl Brantley remembered.

"When we finally got the ball back on the eight-yard line, with virtually no time on the clock," Bucky Cook, a 1977 Georgia alumnus said, "I remember turning to my date and saying, 'It just wasn't meant to be.'"

Some of the Bulldog partisans could watch no more and decided not to stay for the eulogy and burial of potential SEC and national titles.

"Somebody on the sideline made a comment to me, 'A lot of Georgia people look like they're leaving,'" Buddy Sullivan said. "I looked up and saw a lot of red-shirted people going to the exits. It was not like a mass exodus. Those were probably the people who had given up, just like everybody else."

The same feeling permeated parts of Athens where many unlucky students that didn't make the trip watched the game.

"I was with a collection of business school graduate students and landscape architecture students at DaVinci's Pizza on Baxter Street," Eddy Arial recalls. "There were about 20 of us there for the whole game. We had consumed a large amount of beer earlier and as the game dragged on most of us were getting a little down and sleepy. I remember several of the girls had lost all interest in the game and had laid their heads down on the tables."

Georgia had been down, in precarious situations throughout the 1980 season, but this was different.

"We were in so many close games that year," Joe Happe said. "It just got to the point, where even in the fourth quarter of the games we were losing or it was close, we just had this feeling we were going to

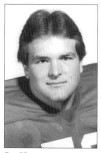

Joe Happe

pull it out. I'll have to be honest, this one was beyond that. We knew we were in trouble."

"We were scared," Buck Belue said after the game. "We hadn't been in that position before this year. We're losing, and we're down to our last two plays."

There was no doubt Georgia was in trouble, but they had reasons to believe.

"We were bummed we put ourselves in that situation," Frank Ros said, "but you still have that hope. I don't think anyone on the sideline was going, 'Oh crap, we've worked this hard and we're going to lose.' I think we felt like we've got to get something done.

"We had hope in multiple areas with a good offense, the best running back and an All-American kicker. All we had to do was get the ball to the 35 or 40 and that's very, very make able on Rex Robinson's part."

Still, some resorted to a higher power.

"My head was on my table praying," said Howard Payne, a UGA student at the time.

While Georgia fans were exuding every ounce of their will upon the grim circumstances, the Florida sideline and players were basking in the glory of certain victory and the sweet taste of a sugary, first-ever SEC title.

"I was on the Florida sidelines when the play happened," said Norm Froscher, who covered the game for the Gainesville Sun. "The Florida players were dancing and carrying on. They thought it was in the bag. They were happy and figured it was over."

Vince Dooley noticed the Florida team, that had been sharp nearly the entire game, did not possess that edge prior to the fatal play.

"In studying the film, I thought there were four or five Florida players that were almost celebrating early," he said. "I knew they were celebrating because one of them was looking over at us trash talking and dancing around. After the first play wasn't successful, the second play was a disaster.

"Had they really been all out (on third down), they might have had a chance to make the tackle. They were not as intense. Now, the player that slipped, that's one thing, but in my estimation, there were some players that didn't react as they had in previous plays. It just did not look like they were into it."

That still infuriates Dock Luckie to this day.

"It was frustrating for me because I was on the sideline (injured)," he said. "I thought all the guys on the field were on the same page, but some of them kind of got lax. I wish I could have been back there playing defensive back. At the time, I was 6-2, 290 pounds and outran most everyone on the football team. I would have been focused and done something to keep that from happening.

"If I had seen our defensive back dancing around on the field, I would have gone over there and knocked him down. I would have hit him so hard he would have rolled about three times. I'm serious. I would have done it and let him know that you don't smile on the football field. You don't mix business with pleasure. Those are the type of people that get touchdowns scored on them. A person should never celebrate until the game is over. That's a sign of weakness, and they took advantage of it."

Ros said it turned out to be poetic justice.

"Some of their defensive backs were already taunting some of our players," he said. "The one that slipped, when Lindsay caught the ball, was one of the ones taunting right before that play. He got what he deserved."

Simply put, Georgia stayed mentally focused and battled till the clock or their opportunities ran out.

"The thing that really stands out in my mind, I think more than anything else, was after the first and second down plays, the clock in the Gator Bowl end zone seemed to be right on top of us, staring in our face," Belue said. "I think Florida relaxed. Florida felt like the game was over. We still had one more play to play."

Herman Hudson, Florida fan

"We were in our seats and one of my buddies said let's go down on the field. Our head coach at Glynn Academy, David McKnight, played at Georgia with Mike Cavan, Jake Scott and that crowd. I said we can't go down of the field. He thought it would be alright and obviously it was as it turned out. We just hopped the fence down in the corner, that's before security got real tight, and put ourselves in the perfect spot to see it all happen.

"No one saw us and no one said a word to us. We were just down there like we knew what we were doing. No credentials whatsoever. There was a lot of media and other people who had the sideline passes and media credentials. We just blended in. It was an awesome situation."

Joe Delany, former SEC official

"With a minute and five seconds to go, Georgia's on their five yard line. They look like they're beat; they've got no chance to win. I'm sure everybody in the stadium felt that way. I'm thinking, I wish this thing would get over with. I've got to go out to dinner tonight."

Buck Belue, Georgia quarterback

"After the second down play, there was some frustration in the huddle. And the Florida players were taunting us, saying, 'It's over.'"

"I was at home, alone, on South Milledge Avenue. My roommate had gone home to Atlanta for the weekend. I had a weekend job at the local Dupont plant, and I was on the 4 p.m. -12 a.m. shift. I had called in to work to say I would be late, having no recollection of the excuse I used, so I could finish watching the game."

—Michael Chidester, '82 Georgia alumnus

Freddy Jones, former Georgia beat writer, The Macon Telegraph

"In my opinion, I think the Florida fans were waiting on something bad to happen. The atmosphere at that time, during that streak with Coach Dooley, was it was just a matter of time."

Hy Dorfman, '82 Georgia alumnus

"On the down prior to the famous play, I looked at my roommate and said, 'Let's get out of here.' Not just out of the stadium but, out of town. We were going back to the motel and grab our stuff before my sister (a Florida student) could get back with her friend and rail on us about how we blew the number one ranking and a shot at the national championship. This was probably not the best idea as we had been indulging at the World's Largest Cocktail party. We collected our cloths and portable bar into bundles and were walking up the aisle from the corner of the end zone Lindsey ran into. I turned and said to my roommate, 'Let's watch one more play before we sprint out of town.'"

Sheila Hoeppner, '83 Georgia alumnus

"I was curled up in the floor in front of the TV with tears in my eyes. We had the volume down on the TV and Larry (Munson) on the radio, typical Bulldog game fashion. Right before the play started, Dad looked at me and said, 'Honey, don't give up on them. I've seen a lot of wild things happen when the Bulldogs look beaten.' At that point, the play started."

THE PLAY: **LEFT 76**

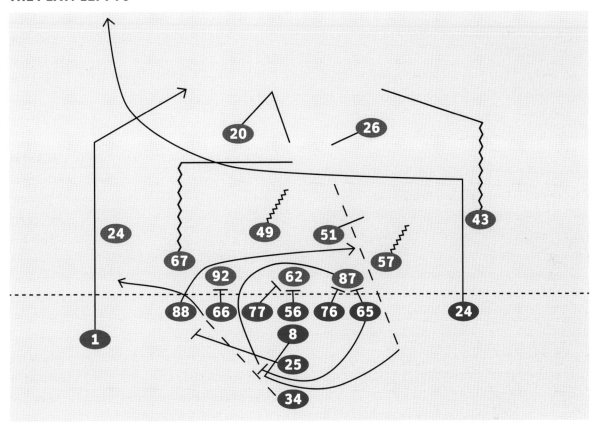

FLORIDA

67 Brown, RE	**49** Jackson, SLB	**24** Knight, RC
(Florida player that slips down)	**51** Little, WLB	**20** Groves, FS
92 Coleman, RT		**26** Curry, SS
62 Whittaker, NG		**43** Gilliam, LC
87 Clark, LT		
57 Golden, LE		

GEORGIA

88 Brown, TE	**8** Belue, QB
66 Harper, LT	**1** Jones, FL
77 Blakewood, LG	**25** Womack, FB
56 Happe, C	**34** Walker, TB
76 Morrison, RG	
65 Hudson, RT	
24 Scott, SE	

With pandemonium and anxiety swirling throughout the Gator Bowl, Georgia needed a composed leader in the huddle. Buck Belue had been in nail biters before.

In 1978, Belue was a heralded freshman out of Valdosta High School in south Georgia. During the year of the Wonderdogs, he saw limited playing time behind junior starter, Jeff Pyburn.

In the last regular season game, against an extremely talented Georgia Tech squad, Belue was inserted with the Bulldogs down 20-0 late in the second quarter. The two-sport star (football and baseball) quickly led Georgia on its first scoring drive to stem the tide and cut the deficit to 20-7.

Trailing 28-21 with just under six minutes left in the game, Belue held the reins of the Georgia offense again, possibly for the last time. He guided the Bulldogs into Georgia Tech territory but faced fourth and three with only 2:36 on the clock.

His youthfulness did not show in such a demanding situation. Under heavy Yellow Jacket pressure, Belue coolly hit a wide open Amp Arnold for the touchdown to make it 28-27. Vince Dooley decided to go for two and the win. After Tech was called for an interference penalty on the first try, Sanford Stadium was a powder keg of nervous energy waiting to explode in either Gold and White or Red and Black.

Belue remained calm. Running an option play toward the Georgia sidelines, the freshmen faked the dive and with Tech defenders hanging on him, pitched to Arnold, who had circled around, for the conversion and an exhilarating come from behind 29-28 victory.

This current situation was not unplowed ground for Belue, but, it was certainly a much different tract of land.

"We were backed up in the Florida end zone, and they were going crazy," Joe Happe remembered. "It was critical for Buck to take ownership of the huddle. I called the huddle, and then we looked to him for the play.

"Buck said, 'Offensive linemen, just block your guy, give me some time and let's try to make something happen.' It is one thing to say a play, but it's another thing to give us eye contact and take charge. It didn't get rid of the pressure. We were in trouble and needed a big play. It helped for him to take charge. That's exactly what he did. Buck was a good quarterback, good leader."

Frank Tilton knew Belue had all the intangibles needed in this kind of atmosphere.

"Buck Belue was a leader," he said. "He won at quarterback at Georgia because he had the charisma and leadership. As far as his talent, Buck was a good player. He was not a great player, but he was a great winner."

With only two plays left to gain a first down and keep their dream alive, Georgia offensive coordinator George Haffner called Left 76.

"I noticed that they were playing a real deep zone, a preventive zone to keep us from completing the long pass," Haffner said after the game. "They had a lot of people back there, as many as eight. So, on third down, we decided to go for a possession-type pass. We needed 11 yards and went with a play, when it works right, that's supposed to give us 15 to 18 yards. It's one of our best passes, one of our safest passes."

"We had our down and distance plays picked out and tried to call a play that we could execute to the best of our ability," Charlie Whittemore said. "We were in a desperate situation but did not use a desperate pass. I think it was a play we were very confident in. It had been very successful for us in many other situations."

Whittemore, who called in the plays from the sideline as the "Flasher", said a variation of that play had almost worked earlier in the game.

"We had actually called the same play the series before, but it was Right 66 instead of to the left," he said. "The read that we had was the post pattern trying to hit Chuck Jones. Buck threw the ball, and the Florida safety and corner reacted to Chuck's post. They hit Chuck right about the time the ball got there. If Chuck makes the catch, he would have walked in with a 70 or 80 yard touchdown pass. This set the tone for the next time that we ran the play. Florida's safety was favoring the post because he knew he was beat the time before."

The play gave Belue multiple options to choose from.

"The description of the play had to do with play action or the half-roll," Whittemore said. "It was a left-handed formation, an odd number, so Chuck Jones was the lined up to the left as the flanker and ran the post. Lindsay, the split end, was to the right running the six-pattern or the hash route. The tight end ran a drag."

Jeff Harper said it was tough enough getting the play started.

"Florida was ecstatic," he said, "and it looked like they had stolen the game from us. It was loud, and the bottom line is you couldn't hear the cadence. You just had to watch the ball out of the corner of your eye."

The Florida defense was in "basically a prevent defense" opting out of a new package that had worked all afternoon.

"We were in a basic three-deep, four underneath coverage," said Tim Groves. "My responsibility was to be deep as the deepest receiver. We had put in new pass coverage and had a lot of success with that throughout the game. They called it the Robber Coverage where I disguised as a three-deep. Then, we rotated to a two-deep, and I played the 10-15 yard range. Here it is, third and 11. They're not going to chunk it deep again. Hindsight is 20-20, but maybe it would have been a little different with the other coverage package."

Robin Fisher also wishes things would have been different from his position.

"First down, we stop them," he remembered. "Second down, we stop them. It's third down and 11. (Mike) Bugar, who was the defensive line coach at the time, makes the decision to pull a couple of linemen out and bring fresh legs in. I remember coming out and was mad about it."

Over the next few seconds, Fisher, his teammates and the Orange and Blue clad faithful would experience a myriad of emotions that would rival any kaleidoscope of colors.

At the same time, Larry Munson provided the defining call of his hall of fame career.

> "I didn't see the play develop because I was focused on making sure that my guy wasn't the guy who caused a problem. I can't remember who I blocked, but I knew it wasn't going to be my man to sack Buck. If I had to trip him, if I had to grab him, I was going to do it."
>
> —Jeff Harper, Georgia left tackle

"On the sideline, you could hear a pin drop. Everybody was watching and waiting."
—Tommy Thurson, Georgia linebacker

"Florida was bringing it. They were coming hard."
—Joe Happe, Georgia center

"I remember I was in the press box. The writers would go down on the field with about five minutes left in the game. In a tight game, I don't go down to the field. There's always time to get down there later. Most of the coaches keep the locker room closed anyway for the players to have a little cooling off period.

"The Florida people were celebrating already and the players were dancing on the sideline. The Georgia fans over in the corner, near the St. John's River, were really quiet. I stood up out of my folding chair, and I said, 'I'm going to watch one more play. This is it.' I had already taken one step toward the elevator to ride down from the press box. Then, there it came. I've never heard such a loud noise before or since in that stadium."

— Murray Poole, former sports editor, Brunswick News

"Oh, boy. Buck Belue to Lindsay Scott, a touchdown. It was a play action pass, I still remember it. All we had to do was stop them there. You miss the next one and you know the game is over."

— Mike Shanahan, Florida offensive coordinator, 1980-1983

Munson: Buck back, third down on the eight, in trouble, got a block behind him.

THE BLOCK

"I've gone back on YouTube and looked at the play several times. After reviewing it, we were in a man to man offense which means the guy in front of you is the guy you normally would have to block. Coach Wayne McDuffie, who was one of the top five offensive line coaches in the country at that time, had prepared us for just about every scenario that you could think of.

"My man was in front of me. On Nat Hudson's side, there was a walk up outside linebacker or defensive end standing over him. When the ball was snapped, the standup linebacker or standup defensive end drops back into coverage. I was holding and biting, doing everything I could to my man because he was a War Daddy.

"The down defensive lineman lined up between Tim Morrison and Nat. He looped all the way around our center and guard. When the guy went around on the stunt, there was nobody to block on Morrison's side of the offensive line. The Florida nose guard stayed over Joe Happe. Jim Blakewood, our left guard, blocked down and helped Joe with the nose guard because he didn't have a linebacker come into his area.

"Nat had a better opportunity to make the block because he was a little farther back on the play and had the better angle. At that point, you don't have to think a lot about it. You go on instincts.

"Where would the help come from? It would come from the back side of Nat's shoulder. If you notice, Tim looked at the Florida player, but he was sucked up too much into the line. Nat followed the man all the way around. It was just a smart football play."

—Jeff Harper, Georgia left tackle

Munson: Gonna throw on the run.

"They were in a zone, and I pushed hard off the snap. I break toward the middle of the field and sit down there. The middle of the field was wide open all day. When I sat down, Buck was chased out of the pocket and swung to the right. That put me in front of the linebacker and Buck pointed. I stepped to the left when he signaled to me."

— Lindsay Scott, Georgia split end

"Scott is the primary receiver on this play and I saw him cutting across with David Little (Florida middle linebacker) close to him. I motioned him to move a little further to my left and Little just let him go, into the clear. He just left him open."

— Buck Belue, Georgia quarterback

"Lindsay was supposed to go 15 yards down field and break back toward the inside and stop on the hash. For Buck, the play was designed for him to set between the guard and the tackle on the left side, but he was flushed out of the pocket and moving.

"I've heard Buck say he told Lindsay to move and he moved. Lindsay ran what he was supposed to. If you look at the film, you will see that Lindsay was on the hash when he caught the ball. The fact that Buck scrambled affected the linebackers more than anything else."

— Charlie Whittemore, Georgia wide receiver coach, 1978-1990

"I vividly remember Lindsay Scott catching the ball. Dadgum, here we are with less than a minute to go, and we are winning the game. I remember sitting there (on the Florida bench) thinking, 'I can't believe we did this. We've got this game won; it's over.' Belue scrambled and hit Lindsay Scott on kind of a crossing route. It wasn't a long throw by any stretch."

— Wayne Peace, Florida quarterback

"When the ball was thrown, I was breaking almost straight back to the line of scrimmage. Everybody was breaking on the ball with the right angles. It looked like the way we were converging on Lindsay Scott, there was a chance for a pretty good collision."

— Tim Groves, Florida safety

Munson: Complete to the 25, to the 30. Lindsay Scott 35, 40."

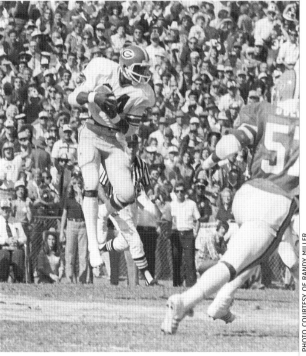

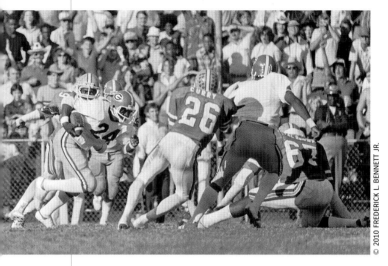

"I distinctly remember Buck wave his arm. The minute he threw the ball, I saw 24 go up for it and come down. I have a vivid memory of Lindsay almost stumbling. I was afraid he was going to go down. I could see straight down the field and knew if one of those linebackers or that cornerback didn't get him, he had clear sailing."

—Sonny Seiler, '56 Georgia alumni/owner of Uga

"I've said many times, when Buck threw the ball and Lindsay caught it, my first reaction was, 'We got it,' which means we got the first down. Now, we can get some momentum and get going."

— Vince Dooley, former Georgia head football coach/athletic director

"When I caught it, I knew I had the first down, but I braced myself to immediately get hit. I tucked it, got my hand down to balance myself and it just opened up."

— Lindsay Scott, Georgia split end

"When Lindsay catches the ball on the right hash, the safety and corner are overcommitted with Chuck on the post and that opened it up for Lindsay down the left sideline and the safety couldn't catch back up with him."

— Charlie Whittemore, Georgia wide receiver coach, 1978-1990

"I couldn't believe it. My whole body went numb. When Lindsay Scott caught the ball, he was two or three steps past the defensive back that was still dancing around. He danced the wrong way and Lindsay went the other way."

— Dock Luckie, Florida defensive tackle

Munson: Lindsay Scott 45, 50, 45, 40. Run Lindsay.

"When he said 'Run Lindsay,' that's exactly like Munson to beg him to run. What's interesting about that is everybody calls that play, run Lindsay run. That's not what he says. He's calling out the yardage and all of a sudden he, real quick, goes 'Run Lindsay.' That's all he said, 'Run Lindsay.' Then he counts the yardage down."

— Tony Barnhart, CBS Sports

"Then he (Scott) came up beside the bench, and I started running with him. I outran him for the first 10-12 yards and then he finally passed me. It was something that we had not planned on."

— Vince Dooley, former Georgia head football coach/athletic director

"Val Brown, who had the outside flat, and Ivory Curry kind of hit and Val slipped a little bit creating a natural running lane for Lindsay. When I saw that opening, I had to totally redirect and make a sharp angle change to get him."
— Tim Groves, Florida safety

"Once I got up the field, I turned on the after burners and let it all hang out. There was no hesitation."
— Lindsay Scott, Georgia split end

"I walked over to the water table after the offense ran the first two plays before Belue to Scott. I wanted to get a quick drink before the next play. While at the table, I saw three high school classmates at the fence flipping me the bird, and yelling how the Gators had ruined our season. We knew (Georgia) Tech had tied Notre Dame. I threw the cup of water at them and as I turned around to go back to the sidelines, I heard the crowd erupt. As I made it to the sidelines, Lindsay ran right by me! I still get goose bumps now!"
— Joe Creamons, Georgia defensive guard

Munson: 25, 20, 15, 10, 5.

"For years, we went to the Georgia-Florida game and it was probably the best seat I've ever had. I was sitting on the 50-yard line about 24-30 rows up. I won't recall the gentleman's name who was sitting right in front of me. He may say he saw that great play, but he was inebriated to say the least. Actually, he was dropped back and his mouth was open. As the touchdown was happening, he never moved because he as totally out of the game, in another land. He was wasted, I guess you would say."
— Bobby Pope, former Mercer University athletic director

"It was like everything opened and Lindsay took off. I remember Tim Groves, our free safety, trying to catch him. Obviously, Tim didn't have a prayer of catching Lindsay."
— Wayne Peace, Florida quarterback

"The scouting report held true. He was a 9.4 sprinter. He hit the sideline and he was gone. I was pretty fast but not 9.4 fast. There was no way I was going to get to him. It just felt like I was running in mud. None of us had the speed of Lindsay Scott."
— Tim Groves, Florida safety

"When I saw him (Scott) get behind everybody, I just couldn't believe it. Typically, in those scenarios, you get everybody back. He's not going to beat you with a first down. You keep everything in front of you and you should be fine. After that game, I think Charlie Lyle finished the season, but I don't think he was the defensive back coach anymore that year."
— Robin Fisher, Florida nose guard

"I can remember sitting there in stunned silence as Lindsay Scott was running down the sideline. I was hoping, looking for a flag somewhere."
Jeremy Foley, Florida athletic director

"I was about six rows up from the bottom so I had a hard time all day seeing anything because everybody had to stand and all the action seemed to be going away from us. All of a sudden, Lindsay Scott is on the outside and he's running toward us. He's got that white jersey on and the silver pants which blended together in the late afternoon sun. So, all you

can see is this red helmet coming at you. All around me, people are starting to realize he's going to score because we can see the angles the Florida defenders at trying to take, and they're not going to catch him. To this day, I can't see the white jersey; I can't see the silver britches; I can see that red helmet coming at me and it's like run, run, run."

— Carl Brantley, Georgia fan

Munson: Lindsay Scott! Lindsay Scott! Lindsay Scott!

"When you're on the sideline, on the field, you do use the feel of the crowd. The roar, the crescendo got more and more and more as he headed down the field. By the time he crossed that goal line, it was a double roar. It was the roar of jubilation from one side but it was also the roar of disappointment and absolute shock from the Florida fans. It was a traumatic moment for both sides."

— Buddy Sullivan, former sports editor Lagrange
   Daily News

"The fact that he (Munson) screamed Lindsay Scott three times, that told you everything you needed to know."

— Tony Barnhart, CBS Sports

© 2010 FREDERICK L. BENNETT JR.

"It must have been a dozen times I took that elevator ride down from the press box with about five or six minutes left in the game thinking, 'Florida is going to win this one.' Very, very often, it didn't happen. 1980 was the epitome.

"I've been lucky enough to see an incredible number of sports events in my 50 years as a journalist. I can't recall another football play that had such a surprising development. Usually, if you break a 93-yard play, it's off a tipped pass or just a hole that cracks open and the guy is in the open after 10 yards. This one, he went 35 or 40 yards before there was any real thought this could go all the way. Georgia was just desperate to get a first down. In that situation, their biggest hope would be to hit a bomb and try a field goal. The chances of that play happening are just infinitesimal."

— Hubert Mizell, former sports editor
   St. Petersburg Times

"There's a typical announcement before every game, 'There will be no cheering in the press box or you will be escorted from the press box.' I think the press box erupted. Let's face it, being a writer you're supposed to be objective, but if you grew up covering Georgia or the Gators, strictly, you're going to be for them. After that play happened, you could take away their sport writer moniker and see who the Georgia fans were."

— Murray Poole, former sports editor Brunswick News

"All press box protocol went out the window. I remember everybody celebrating, a lot of guys crying."

— Greg McGarity, Georgia athletic director

"Four weeks before that game, we had been in a terrible car accident. I had 11 broken ribs, had to have my ruptured spleen removed. In rehabbing, my goal was to get to the Florida game. I still wasn't well enough, but I was determined to go. I'd try to get up and walk a little bit everyday to get my *strength back. Looking back, I should have never done that, but I did. So Vincent had gotten the Jacksonville Bulldog Club to put a trailer in the parking lot in case I couldn't make the whole game. I couldn't, so I went to the trailer and watched the game in the bed. When we scored, I was out of my mind. I looked out of the trailer window and saw a Florida fan take his radio and throw it across the parking lot. It was like he was leaving thinking he had won it, and it didn't happen."*

— Barbara Dooley, wife of former Georgia head
  football coach, Vince Dooley

That wasn't the most famous thing broken at the Gator Bowl on November 8, 1980. As Scott sprinted into legend, Munson was making his legendary call and moments later informed the listening audience of his encounter with some press box furniture.

"Well, I can't believe it," he said. "92 yards and Lindsay really got in a foot race. I broke my chair. I came right through a chair. A metal steel chair with about a five inch cushion, I broke it."

McGarity said considering the dreadful shape the Gator Bowl press box was in, he was not surprised by the incident.

"The chairs back then were old folding chairs with no padding," he said. "I'm sure the bottom of a lot of them was probably about rusted out. What Larry said about, 'I just broke my chair,' really makes sense. People say that really couldn't happen. With the condition the press box was in back then, it makes perfect sense that really happened."

Munson's longtime spotter, Dick Payne, was inches away from the "legendary voice" and said the description given by Munson was completely true.

"I saw the play as clear as a bell," he remembered. "I didn't use field glasses when Georgia was on offense. I used field glasses when they were on defense because I wanted to see who was making the hit.

The Georgia team is to our left, and I'm sitting directly to Munson's left. What I remember, distinctly, is watching Nat Hudson knock that defensive end away from (Buck) Belue. He was free as a bird after Hudson's block.

"What did I do as a spotter on that play? I indicated to Munson, on our board, that Scott was going downfield. I pointed to Hudson when he made the block, that's why Munson was instantly able to call that out. Other than that, there wasn't really anything to call. Munson knew Belue had the ball, but I had to point to Hudson and Scott.

"The booth came apart. Munson jumped up, came

Nat Hudson

back down and went right down through his steel chair to the floor. That was the only stop in the action of that call. His head phone and microphone went off his head. Louis (Phillips) is on one side of him; I'm on the other, and we were helping him get up."

After getting Munson back to his feet, Payne and Phillips paid a visit to the Florida coach's booth for a little payback.

"We're out the door pounding on the Florida coach's door," Payne recalled. "We're just screaming and hollering in retribution for what they had done to us just a minute or two before in our booth. Bear in mind, this is two 50-year old guys pounding on the coach's doors. If the Florida coaches wanted to, they could have come out and beat us to death, but none of them did."

If any chairs were broken in the Florida radio booth, it would have been out of frustration and disgust. Those who never heard the live call of the play by Florida announcer Otis Boggs will never hear a recording of it because the broadcast of this game and most from that era in Florida football history are no longer in existence.

Years later, Norm Froscher, who covered the game for the Gainesville Sun, described the unenviable task Boggs had behind the Gator mike. He wrote:

"His (Munson's) counterpart, Florida's Otis Boggs, tried manfully to detail the Gator disaster. IT was like reporting on the Hindenburg from alongside the helmsman in the gondola or having a microphone next to Casey Jones on the Ol' 97."

MEMORIES

Dick Payne, former Georgia radio spotter

"In a situation like that, the consistency of our crew being together helped make the call of the play as smooth as it was. Munson knew exactly where to look for what I was going to point out to him. He knew exactly where to look for what Louis (Phillips) was going to point out. We had our signals down so well there was no problem, no delay in calling the action. It was a really, really smooth team."

Sheila Hoeppner, '83 Georgia alumnus

"We both jumped to our feet, I was screaming, and crying. The tears really started falling, but they were happy tears, needless to say. My dad was laughing, and saying, 'See, I told you not to give up on them yet!'"

Carl Brantley, Georgia fan

"During the game, I saw a few Florida fans where we were. After the play, I didn't see anybody but white, red and silver. Somehow, they got out of that section pretty quick."

Mike Shanahan, Florida offensive coordinator, 1980-1983

"When you look back, you kind of appreciate the job that Belue and Scott did. They made a play when they had to make it when all the chips were on the line. That was just a great play by two guys keeping their poise. Who knew at that point that would be the difference in them winning the national championship?"

Hubert Mizell, former sports editor St. Petersburg Times

"Among thousands of Florida-Georgia plays since the birth of the match up, one stands higher than all the rest. Buck Belue's little pass across the middle to Lindsay Scott that stunningly evolved into an 93-yard monster touchdown as the Gator Bowl clock was dying. A spectacular Bulldogs season had crawled out of a Jacksonville grave, heroically perpetuated as a Red-and-Black stake was being driven into Gator hearts."

Herman Hudson, Florida fan

"Georgia had just dominated for so many years, and it looked like we were finally going to escape and win one. It was such a let-down. I just stood there, and I'm sure all the other Florida fans had the same feeling. You just stood there in amazement. The game was about to be over and one big play, it's hard to describe. It happened so fast. It just took all the air out of the whole stadium on the Florida side."

Cris Collinsworth, Florida flanker

"Take away the 72 yard touchdown run by Walker and Scott's 93 yard touchdown run, and we would have beaten them in a rout."

Herman Hudson, Florida fan

"We see this play develop with Lindsay running the crossing route. One of the linebackers bit and left an opening for Buck Belue to hit him. From our vantage point, we couldn't tell how far down the field Lindsay was when he completed the pass.

"The noise seemed to build after he caught the ball. The people could tell how it was developing and what was about to happen. When he turned the corner, heading right at us, the whole place went crazy. You could tell no one was going to catch him and he was going to score.

"All of our guys were standing down there, and I was standing with my arms crossed and a cushion under both arms. I think I was probably the closest Gator to Lindsay by the end of the play. You can see us on that film. There have been so many people who saw me and my coaching buddies down there.

"As Lindsay scored, I think David (McKnight) was the first one to grab him. About that time, the Georgia players made a big pile and then a friend of mine, Fred Alexander, reached over and grabbed Lindsay by the hand and said, 'Great catch, Lindsay.' He actually helped him up off the ground."

Florida Fan Herman Hudson

Sonny Seiler

Florida DB Ivory Curry

Florida DB Sonny Gilliam

Jack Peng

Charles Seiler and date

UGA SE Lindsay Scott

WSB-TVs Football Maniac mascot

e Judge Joe Delany

UGA Flanker Chuck Jones

UGA cheerleader Jim Brown

PHOTO COURTESY OF HARGRETT RARE BOOK & MANUSCRIPT LIBRARY/UNIVERSITY OF GEORGIA

THE OFFICIAL'S PERSPECTIVES

Bobby Gaston, former SEC official

"Every official actually has a key on pass plays. The two wing officials, the two deep officials on the sidelines, and the deep official in the middle. That's five officials and five eligible receivers. Each one has a charged receiver at the snap. You stay with him in his original moves as your key. Then, it becomes zone if the ball comes your way. You watch your man to make sure he doesn't pick or that he doesn't get held along the way. Last but not least, you go to ball. We try to have at least three sets of eyes watching the ball as it comes in. It's what we call, triangulate. It helps us to make sure that the pass is legal and there is not any interference by either player. The rotation begins once the ball is caught.

"I was on the Georgia sideline that entire day. Lindsay Scott was on the opposite side of the formation from me. My duties at the snap are to move down about two yards watching the tackle on my side to make sure he doesn't hold. My key is the nearest receiver to me. He didn't seem to be involved and I got off the tackle. Suddenly, I realized that Lindsay was cutting across the field. The officials on the far sideline started to move across the field toward the ball. They were watching for any possible clips or other actions that would create a foul or cut down the defensive pursuit.

"As Lindsay made a cut, the defender slipped and went down. Lindsay made the turn and then it was the question of whether or not the Florida defenders could get to him. He headed towards me and my sideline and then turned and made the run the rest of the way. My position at that stage is to stay with the ball carrier and watch him.

"Joe Delaney (side judge) was downfield from me about 10 to 15 yards, and he moved toward us and watched for blocks in the middle of the field to make sure there were no clips.

"I probably got as far as the 20 yard line when he went across the goal line. Delaney was about five yards behind him when Lindsay scored. As an official, you're really not aware of players or anything else. You're aware of keys that you're assigned to. You don't normally get wrapped up in the game itself, but in that case, you couldn't help but be wrapped up in it because it was such an explosive act."

Joe Delany, former SEC official

"I'm the deep official, and my perspective was different from Bobby Gaston's. I had the middle of the field all the way to my sideline. I'm seeing the receiver and the defensive backs at the same time, looking for pass interference or anything that might be going on illegally. If it (the play) was going to the other side, I would rotate toward the middle of the field. That's really the way I thought the play was going until the defensive backs collide and Lindsay cuts out to my side. Once he cut back to my sideline, he was wide open. Nobody had a chance to catch him."

A REPORTER'S DASH TO IMMORTALITY

Freddy Jones, former Georgia beat writer,
The Macon Telegraph

"I thought it was going to be one of the worst days in my life. Georgia was my beat, and I was writing the lead story that day (for the Macon Telegraph) which meant I had the game story. Having the game story, you're going to go in the locker room of the winning team. I was actually on the Florida sideline because I would have gone from the Florida sideline, through the portal to get to the Florida dressing room.

"I'm trying to get my questions together and go back to being objective. I'm trying to forget about the game and get ready for the story. At the time, their players, they thought they had the ballgame won. They were yelling on the field. I guess encouragement might be how you'd state it. Every time they would make a play, they would lift their helmets and shake them in the air. The cheerleaders were high-fivin'. They thought they had the ballgame won. I thought they had the ballgame won.

"I'm watching the play, and I see Buck scramble. Then he got rid of the ball and I see Lindsay. I'm still not excited about the play because I'm assuming they've got enough people around that he might get 10 or 15 yards. Then, Georgia's going to have to go 80 yards.

"One guy misses and Lindsay heads toward the sideline. That was the opposite sideline and the opposite corner from where I was. I'm trying to get a better view of the play, and here he comes down the sidelines. I'm at the 20. I'm trying to not get blocked because the people on the sideline were looking and stretching. I'm at the 20, and I get into a little trot. I'm going toward the end zone, the opposite corner of where Lindsay would eventually end up. I don't think he's going to be caught. It looks to me like, dawggone it, he's going to score.

"So, I break into a full run. I'm watching the play and I'm thinking, 'Hey, I've got to get to the other side. I'm going to have to get into that dressing room.' More than that, I'm wrapped up in the moment. Again, it might have been one of my darker days in journalism, but, I grew up with this.

"I've got the little note pad in my hand, and I am in a full dash. I figured I had a good 20 yards from the Florida sideline to the end zone. I turned in one hell of a time for 75 yards (55 for the width of the field). It wasn't clocked but I believe that I would have qualified for the heat race.

"He (Scott) is going down the sideline; I'm going down to the corner. He gets into the corner, and I'm still behind the line where the press usually stands. The pile moves farther back into the end zone, and I've lost it by then. How I got into the middle of that pile, I cannot tell you. But I was in the middle of the pile.

"Everybody's jumping up and down, and I felt somebody's helmet hit me. I look and there's a little bit of blood on top of my head. That's what made Erk Russell famous. I'm feeling pretty good. Everybody's slappin' and huggin'. I just had to wait till they quit because I'm in the pile. I'm in the huddle. I probably didn't weigh 150 pounds. There's no way I was going to break out of that pile so I just hugged with the best of them.

"As the huddle broke, I realized the official had thrown a flag. I knew what it was for.

"As Coach Dooley tells the story, when he was looking at the film trying to find out who was the cause of the penalty, he sees me in the middle of the pile. He has always made the statement if that penalty had cost Georgia the game, I would have never worked for the (University of Georgia) athletic association. So instead of having 21 years at Georgia, I don't know where I would have been. Later, I saw the highlight and I'm saying, 'That's my dumb butt in that huddle.'"

16 Ecstasy and Agony

The reaction following the Belue to Scott miracle was like the fans in the stands themselves...at opposite ends of the spectrum. It was night and day, black and white, hot and cold, on and off...Ecstasy and Agony.

BULLDOG ECSTASY

Buck Belue, Georgia quarterback
"I was collapsed on the 50 yard line like a 12 year old kid kicking my feet on the ground as the ground trembled. Just a great feeling."

Carl Brantley, Georgia fan
"In the stands, people you may have said a few words to during the game like, 'hello' or 'where are you from', all of a sudden, we all became best friends. This lady behind me starts kissing everybody. She didn't care if you were a man or a woman; if you were married or not. She pulls out a fifth of Jack Daniels, opens it and starts passing it around. People who don't even drink are taking hits off this because they are so happy."

Tommy Thurson, Georgia linebacker
"When he (Lindsay) hit the end zone, we all just ran. I was about midway in between everyone and got smashed a few times."

Jeff Harper, Georgia left tackle
"I didn't realize Lindsay was going to score until he crossed the goal line. Then my focus was just get down there, got down there, get down there. I was a very emotional, intense type of football player. When I got down there, I was a little over the top. I ran into Frank Ros and about beat the crap out of him because I was so excited. You go back to that controlled environment you play in on the play, and then once you get down there, you just let it all go."

Tony Barnhart, CBS Sports
"I stayed in my little room in the Ocono Lodge in Tallahassee watching the game. When Buck Belue hit Lindsay Scott and Lindsay took it the distance, I jumped out of my chair and put my fist through a hanging lamp and absolutely destroyed it."

"We were up in the press box and really in the jar because we saw the perfect season going down the tubes. It was one of these surreal experiences where you couldn't believe it was happening. I'll never forget my wife, Cheryl, was sitting below the press box, and she knew where we were sitting during the game. After we scored, I remember sticking my head out of there and was shaking my head in disbelief. It was one of those plays where certain things had to fall Georgia's way. Probably the biggest play in the history of Georgia football."
— Greg McGarity, Georgia athletic director

Michael Chidester, '82 Georgia alumnus

"I was feeling pretty bummed as it looked like we were going to finally lose a game and, on top of that, I was losing money. I was watching it with (Larry) Munson on the radio and the TV sound turned down. When Lindsay caught that ball and that Florida back fell down, I jumped up off the couch, punching my fist in the air, resulting in a hole in the living room ceiling."

Preston Martin, '75 Georgia alumnus

"I was in the corner of the Gator Bowl where Lindsay scored. I had just poured a fresh Coke and something, feeling so dejected. When he scored, the newly poured cup went high above my head, as many others did and nobody seemed to care."

Troy Schmidt, '84 Georgia alumnus

"The campus was pretty empty since it was an away game. I was a freshman watching the game in the Russell Hall TV lounge with a bunch of friends from my floor.

"I remember all of us sitting on the edge of our seats, nervously fidgeting as the ball was snapped. As the pass flew into the air and landed squarely in Lindsay Scott's arms, the room erupted. I never have been a part of such mania before, nor since. We hugged and cheered and then began to tear the room apart. Chairs went flying. Tables overturned. Our hugs turned into a huge pile up of bodies in the middle of the floor. I'm a relatively calm guy, but that moment will forever be defined as my craziest."

Mark E. Murphy, '84 Georgia alumnus

"I was a freshman at Georgia that season and elected not to go to the game (a decision I'll regret for the rest of my life) because I didn't have a ticket or the

Lindsay Scott to Mrs. Scott Lindsay
Karen Morgan '86 Georgia alumnus

"I was born and raised in Athens and began going to Georgia games in mom's uterus. I looked at my birthday on the calendar and did the math. I was conceived before, during or after the 1963 Georgia-Florida game.

"On November 8, 1980, I was 16 years old and in Athens Regional Hospital, then Athens General, with pneumonia and a collapsed lung. On that day, most of the televisions were turned to the game. People may have been sick, but they certainly weren't dead, and there was a ballgame to watch. When Buck Belue threw the pass to Lindsay Scott, you could hear cheering throughout the hospital. One of the cardiologists was sprinting down the hallway. We thought someone was coding but then we realized that the doctor was running and cheering as Lindsay ran down the field while Larry Munson yelled those infamous words, 'Lindsay Scott, Lindsay Scott, Lindsay Scott.'

"Fast forward 15 years later. I was visiting Maine in 1995 where I met a handsome young man on a blind date. His name was Scott Lindsay. I told him the story about Lindsay Scott and the Georgia-Florida game of 1980. Although he lived in Boston, Massachusetts, he had actually watched it on television! He told me he had always wanted to go to an SEC football game. Two months later, I took him to the Georgia-Florida game. We were married within the year, so now I am Mrs. Scott Lindsay. And I have a t-shirt with Larry Munson's 1980 call hanging in our home."

means to purchase one. Instead, I went home to Savannah and watched the game with my girlfriend Daphne, who I later married.

"When Lindsay Scott caught that pass, I was simply hoping for a first down. I soon realized that he had a chance to gain more—a *lot* more. I had Munson's radio broadcast turned up full blast. As Larry screamed 'Lindsay Scott! Lindsay Scott! Lindsay Scott!' I jumped up into the air, slipped and cracked my head against my mother-in-law's terrazzo floor. I watched the rest of the pandemonium from there with a knot on my head and with unbridled elation in my heart. After that, I didn't miss another Georgia-Florida game for more than ten years."

Frank Ros, Georgia linebacker

"I ran all the way down there (to the end zone). If you look at the film, I have the helmet in my hand. When we got to the pile, Jeff Harper came flying in with his helmet on and was head butting me. I quickly caught myself and said 'Oh Lord, I've got to get out of here.'"

Edward (Eddy) Ariail, '82 Georgia alumnus

"When the play happened, needless to say the place (DaVinci's Pizza-Athens, Ga.) went crazy. People were standing on tables and chairs, and the cheering was so loud we actually never heard Munson's famous call once the ball was caught by Lindsay Scott."

"Don't you think that's rather severe?"
Bobby Gaston, former SEC football official

"When he scored, the Georgia bench came unglued, came down the sideline and went into the end zone. It was at that time that I realized that we were going to have a foul for excessive celebration. It was totally chaotic, not only the players and coaches, but the people in the end zone. There were people from everywhere that got in on that stack. It was obvious, as far as the foul was concerned. Then I moved on down to about the 10 yard line and threw the marker.

"Once I started back, Coach Dooley met me and wanted to know exactly what the problem was. I told him, 'Coach, your players left their team area and that's a foul.' He said, 'What does that mean?' And I said, 'What it means is we're going to have to put a 15-yard penalty on you on the kickoff.' His response

to that was, 'Don't you think that's rather severe?' You couldn't do anything but laugh, there. It was severe because the ball was kicked off in those days from the 40 which meant it would be kicked off from the 25 with the penalty.

"Coach Dooley was a very cool customer, and he knew what the penalty was for. He was a coach that really maintained his cool on the sideline. I think he just threw it out there. As an official, you try to be as cool and efficient as you can. You try not to show excitement even though there may be some. When talking to a coach, you stand at parade rest so your hands are behind you and you are not confronting the coach. You try to make it as professional and as comfortable as you can for both parties."

Dr. David Kent, Georgia fan

"We were having a football afternoon in Augusta at the Medical College of Georgia watching the game and biting our nails. Someone had an old rickety house and we were out on the porch with an old Zenith box TV propped up and adequate refreshments.

"It was third down, and we were thinking this is not looking good. The next thing you know, everybody threw their beer up and were screaming and yelling. The TV almost fell off the porch, and we made quite a ruckus."

Charles Seiler, '83 Georgia alumnus

"I think I had red slacks and a white shirt on and was right behind the flag in the corner of the end zone with my girl friend. If you look at the replay, there was a million cups and crap thrown onto the field. I remember somebody threw a big liquor bottle onto the field and even with that place going so crazy, I heard it whistle over my head."

GATOR AGONY

Mike Bugar, Florida defensive line coach, 1980-1982

"It seemed like somebody let the air out, just punched you in the gut. You just couldn't breathe because you could not believe that actually was happening. We were in a state of shock on the sideline. We had them beat, obviously."

Tim Groves, Florida safety

"Just disbelief. Man, we had never won an SEC title, ever, and here we were one play away. We were right there to do it and it just ripped your heart out. Good gracious, it was right there for us. Just goes to show, you've got to play every play like it's the last."

Robin Fisher, Florida nose guard

"Charley (Pell) was a heavy smoker. Knowing Charley, I gotta believe he probably had to light one or two up in disbelief."

Dock Luckie, Florida defensive tackle

"I was so shocked, someone could have thrown an object from the stands and hit me, and I wouldn't have ever felt it."

Wayne Peace, Florida quarterback

"I was sitting beside Tyrone Young and James Jones on the bench and literally having that feeling of, 'What just happened?'"

Tyrone Young, Florida flanker

"I remember when I was in the sixth or seventh grade, and I was watching the Gators on television. And they were talking about that team having a chance to win an SEC championship. Here I was right in the middle of it today. And it just slipped away from us."

Sonny Gilliam, Florida cornerback

"We didn't make the big turnover at the right time. I just can't believe it. I just can't. But, you know, Georgia is the No. 2 team in the nation and great teams are supposed to make plays like that."

Herman Hudson, Florida fan

"I'm sure the Georgia people had not given up, but they knew what was about to happen. They were going to lose the game. On the other hand, the Florida fans knew they were about to win one. One side went from happy to sad and the other side went from sad to happy, pretty quick."

James Jones, Florida fullback

"I was watching and crying at the same time."

17 "The band just played on and on"

Florida was still assured of good field position due to Georgia's excessive celebration penalty.

"After emotions settled down," Carl Brantley said, "we have to kick off to them. We thought we had it won, but after what Florida had just been through, we were like 'No, just wait.' There was a little bit of apprehension."

The Gators started at their own 36-yard line with 59 seconds left. With its quick strike offense, that had riddled the Georgia defense in the second half, that was certainly enough time to generate a good opportunity to score.

Georgia fan Harry Kicklighter said even the Florida partisans found it difficult to muster up hope for their own miracle.

"It was quiet," he said. "The Florida fans were just shocked. Even when Florida had the ball after we scored, all the air was gone out of their sails."

It took one play for those sails to be ripped from the yardarm, thus, setting Florida adrift for another year in the sea of "What Might Have Been."

Attempting to hit Tyrone Young across the middle, Wayne Peace overthrew him and was intercepted by Mike Fisher, his second pick of the day.

"You'll talk to a lot of players and they can remember every play of every game," Peace said. "I'm not that way at all. But, to this day, the only thing that comes to my mind that I felt like was a blown opportunity (for Florida) is after Georgia scored and we got the ball back.

"We went back out on the field, and I promptly threw an interception. I remember thinking I had a great game, we played well and after their big play, when Florida needed me the most, I go out and throw an interception. That's the play that really bothers me."

Munson counted down the final seconds as only he could.

"Look at the clock. Will you look at that clock? Gone. Beaten. Knocked out of the ranks of the unbeaten. Not throwing sharp all day and there it was to Lindsay down the middle for roughly 20 or 25 and off he went. Seven, six, five, four, three, two, one...Dogs have won it 26-21. Pandemonium here. Georgia's won it by five points when the Gators had it in the pocket and the zipper had closed.

"26-21, Georgia's defeated Florida. Shockingly, stunningly unbelievable."

PHOTO COURTESY OF WINGATE DOWNS

MEANWHILE BACK IN ATLANTA...

As the teams left the field, and ABC was concluding its broadcast, it showed that No. 1 Notre Dame had tied Georgia Tech 3-3, late in the fourth quarter. The Yellow Jackets hung on for the tie thus serving as the death-nail for the top-ranked Irish and the catapult for its hated foe, the second-ranked Bulldogs.

"We got into the locker room and we found out, at least I did, that Tech tied Notre Dame," Frank Ros said. "We were going to move up and that added fuel to the excitement."

In stark contrast was the shock among the Gator players as they left the field.

"When the game was over," Joe Happe remembered, "and we met to shake hands, Cris Collinsworth was walking across the field staring off into the distance, just shaking his head. He didn't say a word."

Most Florida fans didn't stay long either.

"When the game was truly over," said Sonny Seiler, "I can remember seeing the Florida fans evacuate the stands like a bomb had hit their side."

On the opposite side, it was paradise.

"I know I stayed in the stadium at least 45 minutes," Brantley said. "The band just played on and on. They never stopped. There were some people behind us who were in their 80s and had been going to the Georgia-Florida game for years. The biggest thing I remember was one man crying huge tears. He said, 'This is the happiest day of my life.'"

Squab

Frank Tilton, former sports editor
Savannah Morning News

"After the game was over, we made our way to the locker room. They kept us waiting outside a little bit longer than normal. The fans were about to tear that old stadium down. We couldn't even think it was so loud.

"All of a sudden, this guy came walking up with a big cowboy hat and said, 'I'm Buck Belue's dad.' Guarding the door, with a mean disposition, was the trainer, Squab Jones. He was old but you didn't want to mess with him. Squab shoved him and shoved all of us. I'll never forget it. He said, 'nobody's getting in here until Coach Dooley says you can get in.' As soon as they opened the door and we could get past Squab, we ran as fast as we could to Lindsay Scott."

Squab Jones worked over 70 years for UGA.

MEMORIES

Joe Creamons, Georgia defensive guard

"Right after the game, I met two guys in the middle of the field I had played against in high school. Bubba Pratt had played linebacker for Florida and graduated in 1979. John Whittaker was a junior nose guard. We shook hands, and I vividly remember Bubba saying, 'Y'all are the luckiest son-of-a-b&%$# in the world and if we did not beat y'all today, we may never beat y'all!'! To that I replied, 'Bubba, tell ya what Erk (Russell) tells us...I'd rather be lucky than good.' With that, we all headed to our locker rooms."

Freddy Jones, former Georgia beat writer, The Macon Telegraph

"It was frenzied because the majority of the fans were drunk. That's when it really was the World's Largest Outdoor Cocktail Party. They couldn't believe what they had seen. You've got to remember, the Florida people were waiting on something bad to happen. The Georgia people were waiting on something good to happen and they got it."

Barbara Dooley, wife of former Georgia head football coach, Vince Dooley

"Outside the locker room was euphoric. Everybody was happy, screaming and yelling. It was such an emotional victory because we were down and out. It was truly over. All of a sudden it was like the sky opened and Jesus appeared. It was a miracle."

© 2010 FREDERICK L. BENNETT JR.

Wayne Peace, Florida quarterback

"After the game, everybody was saying you guys played so well. Hold your head up; be proud. It was just devastation. As a team, I was happy we played so well, but when you have a chance to knock off a team of that stature, you have to put them away. They won the game, we lost the game and they deserve all the credit. Now that I'm old, fat and bald, you definitely remember the hurt."

George Haffner, Georgia offensive coordinator, 1980-1990

"We sent out our best receiver and Buck did a great job directing him into the open field and then getting the ball to him. Don't give credit to me for calling the play. Give the credit to the players for executing so well."

18 Georgia Jubilation and Gator Grief

If ecstasy and agony are conditions of the moment, then jubilation and grief followed Georgia and Florida into their locker rooms and to their respective campuses.

"When everybody rushes to the dressing room, it was one of the greatest sites I've ever seen," Freddy Jones recalled. "I saw a lot of big, big linemen hugging and dancing with each other. I was in the locker room after the national championship; I don't think it matched the Florida win at all."

Georgia's starting left tackle was overcome by the moment.

"After the game, I can remember going into the locker room and just crying," said Jeff Harper, "sitting down and having tears because of the emotion and what was going on."

The normally reserved coaching staff even let loose.

Jeff Harper

"What was different was the coach's excitement in the locker room was over the top," Joe Happe remembered. "Normally, they are very reserved and under control, but they were unbelievably excited, especially my offensive line coach, Wayne McDuffie. He had a reputation in the industry of being the toughest SOB out there. He wasn't jumping up and down going crazy, but his face was lit up and he kept saying over and over again, 'What great character.'"

The decibel level across the field was non-existent. Florida was grieving as another shot at a SEC title was laid to rest beneath the Gator Bowl gridiron.

When asked if he had ever suffered a tougher defeat, Mike Shanahan's response was simply, "No."

"To get beat like that, nobody said a word in the locker room," Mike Bugar said. "We had the game won, we really did."

Charley Pell was still at a loss to how his team got beat on such a routine play.

"How many ways can you describe a simple curl pattern on which the guy just outran everybody," he asked. "It took a circus play, or we would have upset the No. 2 team in the country."

He also pointed to one simple factor.

"One of the four things we had to do to win was have our secondary tackle well," Pell said. "And they did except for the first series and the last series. Of course, you have to give credit to Georgia too. Herschel's a great running back and they have a great football team."

The loss might have cut Florida's senior, All-American wide receiver the deepest. The pain and disappointment was clearly heard in Cris Collinsworth's voice: "It just ain't right. We kicked their butts."

"That was a fluke," he told reporters. "I don't care what you say. We had them beaten. They had two plays for over 70 yards, and they beat us...I don't know...it's ridiculous."

Above the locker rooms, a party and wake was occurring simultaneously. Georgia fans were creating an uproar never heard before in the Gator Bowl.

"The Georgia folks were above where we were going into the dressing room, and they were just stomping and bringing that place down," Jones said. "When you got into the dressing room, you could hear that thunder. It was kind of scary. You didn't know what was going to happen to that place. I've heard louder crowds, but I don't know I've ever heard that eerie, thunderous type stomping. I've never heard that since."

Sullivan attributes it to all the elements of the perfect storm coming together.

"After the interviews, I was struck by how many Georgia people were there," he said. "The band was still playing. The fans were still there. I had never seen anything quite like this before.

"It was a combination of the play, the moment, the consequences of the game, the fact that it was Georgia-Florida, and the number one ranking that everybody knew was coming. You add all of that up and it was just absolute pandemonium among Georgia people. In the history of Georgia football, there's never been a Saturday afternoon quite like that one."

Florida fans could probably say the same thing. As Georgia's Redcoat Marching Band pounded out victorious tunes of exultation, a dirge of defeat played for the Gators.

"After I left the Georgia locker room," Jones said, "I remember seeing some of the Florida players sitting up against the wall outside their locker room and dejected, obviously. Some of them still hadn't gotten dressed. It was a disaster. For the few Florida fans that remained in the stands, their heads were in their laps. Their hands were covering their heads. They just couldn't believe it."

The numbness from such a devastating loss made Florida's short, 71 mile drive back to Gainesville the longest ride they had ever experienced, especially for Robin Fisher.

"We were in shock and disbelief," he said. "I remember getting on the bus and dipping for the first time in my life. I did that because Kyle Knight said, 'Here Fish, you need a dip.' I took one and got so darn sick, I threw up almost all the way home."

Dock Luckie was beside himself.

"I didn't cool down when were on the bus going home," he said. "A guy gave me an apple, and the next thing I knew, I was making apple juice. When we got back to campus, I went straight to the weight room and worked out. I also went out and picked up some

Everyone celebrated Georgia's miracle win.

Man of the moment—Lindsay Scott.

cars. I wore myself out mentally and physically, and then went into the stadium (Florida Field, a.k.a. The Swamp) and fell asleep. I think I slept there all night."

In Athens, Ga., there was very little sleep. It was the new capital of college football. A crowd of fans welcomed their heroes at McWhorter Hall chanting, "We're number one." Some even remembered to thank Georgia's unlikely ally shouting, "Let's hear it for the Jackets."

The Classic City was engulfed in celebration. Its streets were anything but quiet.

"Driving down Lumpkin, right in the middle of the road," said William Rhangos, a Georgia student, "we saw about 35 delirious KAs. They were raising hell and congratulating everything and everybody that drove by."

Kim Iocovozzi and Virginia Anderson of the Athens Banner Herald reported:

"Word spread quickly that a party at a downtown bar was the place to go, and by 10:30 p.m., everybody was bouncing off the walls. The country music band's lead singer kept yelling, 'HOW BOUT THEM DAMN DOGS!'"

PHOTO COURTESY OF WILLIAM WINBURN

MEMORIES

Tim Groves, Florida safety

"It could never happen again in a million years."

Cris Collinsworth, Florida flanker

"I was wishing the gopher would stand up and stop him." (Reference to the gopher in the movie *Caddy Shack* that debuted in 1980)

Edward (Eddy) Ariail, '82 Georgia alumnus

"Another memory I still have from the Florida game is on Saturday evening and Sunday, seeing the cars at a car dealership that was on the Atlanta Highway where it intersects with Beechwood. I don't remember the name of the dealership, and I believe a hotel is there now. But, they had painted a single letter across the windshield of each car so the cars spelled out — G-R-E-A-T S-C-O-T-T."

Mike Shanahan, Florida offensive coordinator, 1980-1983

"I remember the ride home from that game. We were so disappointed because we had so much respect for Georgia and they were such a good football team. We had the opportunity to get it done and we didn't. You remember those games a lot more than you do wins, the ones that got away from you when you thought you had the game under control."

Tyrone Young, Florida flanker

"What I did is now unimportant. Only thing I can see is Lindsay Scott running free. It'll haunt us all."

19 The Headlines

Belue-to-Scott Desperation Pass Saves 'Dogs From Jaws of Gators

JACKSONVILLE, Fla.
(AP) — Herschel Walker,
Georgia's fabulous fresh-
shocked Florida with
down burst

The Atlanta Journal
THE ATLANTA CONSTITUTION
SUNDAY, NOVEMBER 9, 1980

In two sections today

Sports

SECTION D

Georgia turns back Florida, 26-21; Tech stuns No. 1 Notre Dame, 3-3

Daytona Beach
Sunday News-Journal **SPORTS**

C

NOVEMBER 9, 1980

Great Scott! 'Dogs Pull It Out

Rome News-Tribune **Sports**   *Area* / *State* / *National*   Section C

SUNDAY NOV 9 1980

Tech ties Notre Dame, 3-3; Dogs to benefit?

Yellow Jackets stun No. 1 ranked Irish

ATLANTA (AP) — Notre Dame failed to play to its
billing as the top-ranked college football team in the nation
Saturday in a stunning 3-3 tie against inspired Georgia Tech
and Irish coach Dan Devine sounded more like a loser.
This isn't the easiest press conference I've ever attended,"
said Devine moments after his Irish were shocked by a Yellow
Jacket defense that

No. 2 Georgia rallies by Florida

JACKSONVILLE, Fla. (UPI) — With less than two minutes
to go Saturday and Florida on the verge of upsetting second
ranked Georgia, Lindsay Scott pulled in a Buck Belue pass and
out raced a phalanx of Florida defenders for a 93-yard
touchdown.

The New York Times

SPORTS

Section **5**

Sunday, November 9, 1980

Notre Dame Tied; Georgia Is Victor

93-Yard Play Beats Florida

Georgia Tech In 3-3 Deadlock

By GORDON S. WHITE Jr.
New York Times

Sports

Gainesville Sun

section D

Sunday, Nov. 9, 1980

Gators Come Ohhhhhhhh So Close

By JACK HAIRSTON
Sun Sports Editor

JACKSONVILLE — The University of Georgia left the stadium Saturday with a 26-21 victory and almost certainly the nation's No. 1 ranking of college football, and the University of Florida left with a bitter defeat because of one backward pass from Buck Belue to Lindsay Scott...

Florida Coach Charley Pell said, "All I thought was it was a simple curl pattern. We didn't get beat by any double reverse. When Scott broke free, I wound catch him, even though I thought our safety Tim Groves...

Georgia Coach Vince Dooley was asked if he had ever thought Scott, who's had disciplinary problems at Georgia, might never fulfill his potential.

"Frankly, I did wonder," Dooley said. "But today, I think Lind..."

Georgia Stuns Florida With Last-Minute Win

JACKSONVILLE, Fla. (AP) — "First time in my life I ever pulled for Georgia Tech," one emotionally drained Georgia fan said Saturday as he left the Gator Bowl.

He had just seen the unbeaten, second-ranked Georgia Bulldogs salvage a stirring 26-21 triumph over No. 20 Florida when Lindsay Scott turned a pass from Buck Belue into a game-winning 93-yard touchdown — longest scoring play in Georgia's history — with just 63 seconds left.

Then came the news from Atlanta that lowly Georgia Tech had held No. 1-rated Notre Dame to a scoreless standoff, making the Bulldogs the nation's only unbeaten major-college team. The victory clinched at least a tie for the Southeastern Conference title and can go to the Sugar Bowl by beating or tying Auburn next Saturday.

The big star was Herschel Walker, the fabulous freshman who stole the spotlight by rushing for 238 yards — including a touchdown on a fourth play — and boosted his season Georgia...

record of 1,334 yards on the ground.

Then it was Rex Robinson kicking field goals of 25 and 20 yards in the third period to give Georgia a 20-10 lead and tie the SEC career scoring record of 254 by Louisiana State's Charles Alexander.

Later it was Florida, led by freshman quarterback Wayne Peace, which rallied for 11 points in the final period on James Jones' 11-yard run, Peace's 2-point pass to Tyrone Young and Brian Clark's 40-yard field goal, grabbing a 21-20 lead with 6:52 to play. With Florida utilizing a wide-open attack with two split ends and two slotbacks, Peace passed for 206 yards on 20-of-37 including 10 to Young for 183 yards.

And it looked bleak for the Bulldogs when Florida's Mark Dickert punted out of bounds at the Georgia 8 with 1:35 remaining.

"We were down," Coach Vince Dooley conceded. "I don't think there was any question Florida had the game. But no matter how bad it gets, you've got to hold on and never give up."

And Georgia didn't, even after Belue lost one yard on a scramble and then threw an incomplete pass. All the Bulldogs really wanted was to get in field goal position for Robinson, who connected from 57 and 51 yards out a week ago.

Belue scrambled around for a few seconds, which had the Florida secondary moving up to guard against a run, and then hit Scott at the 26. "A first-down play," Dooley called it.

"I turned around and saw an open field," said Scott. So the junior speedster, who anchors Georgia's 440-yard relay team, angled toward the left sideline and took off for the end zone.

"I let it all hang out," Scott said. "I knew it was about the only chance we had so I just gave it all I had."

Florida Coach Charley Pell called it "a simple curl pattern. It wasn't a double reverse pass, nor was it fancy. The difference between No. 2 in the nation and No. 20 is knowing how to make that last play. We will be back in that situation again some time and then we will make that play."

Miracle Play Saves Georgia

By BUDDY SULLIVAN
Daily News Sports Editor

JACKSONVILLE, Fla.—Buck Belue and Lindsay Scott were only trying to salvage a desperation first down with their team behind by a point with just over a minute to play.

What they did was strike gold on a simple pass play that turned into a 93-yard touchdown that preserved Georgia's undefeated season as the Bulldogs measured the Florida Gators at the tape, 26-21, in an absolutely hellacious college football game Saturday.

Most Georgians, about 34,000 of them in a bulging Gator Bowl crowd of better than 68,000 which was splashed with warm sunshine and a flowing abundance of liquor, had given up.

Georgia's 20-10 third quarter lead had evaporated as Gator freshman quarterback Wayne Peace and receiver Tyrone Young brought 6-1 Florida back into a 21-20 lead with 6:52 to play.

And things looked exceedingly grim when Florida's Mark Dickert punted out of bounds at the Georgia eight-yard line with 1:35 remaining.

"We were really down," Georgia coach Vince Dooley said. "I don't think there was any question Florida had the game. But no matter how bad it gets, you've got to hold on and never give up."

Belue drew out the suspense by waiting until Georgia had third and 11 at the seven after he lost a yard on a scramble then threw an incomplete pass.

All Georgia wanted was a first down to try and get some offensive momentum to position Rex Robinson for a winning field goal.

What transpired was a play called "66 right", a routine pass play involving the wide receiver, Scott in this case, on a simple curl pattern down field.

Scott took off and stopped at the Georgia 25 where he turned around, all alone, waiting for Belue's short pass over the middle. Belue was scrambling to his right under pressure from the Gators before he finally threw back to his left to Scott.

"I couldn't believe I was all alone out there. It scared me," Scott said later in the chaotic...

Georgia Should Climb To No. 1

By HERSCHEL NISSENSON
AP Sports Writer

All Georgia wanted was a...

...tended their unbeaten streak to a school record 28 games. Jeff Quinn threw scoring passes to...

---

114   **Belue to Scott!**

Ah, a Georgia-Florida game for all seasons

As I see it
David Lamm
Times-Union Executive Sports Editor

As improbable as it is that the St. Johns River flows north, such is the nature of this Jacksonville autumn classic known as the Georgia-Florida game.

It is a series of November meetings which dates back to pre-World War I days and clogs the memory with vivid recollections, both sweet and bittersweet but never in between.

That such a contest between young college men, heavily clad in gladiator-like equipment and performing for the pleasure of thousands of spirited (liquid refreshmentional) fans, can create such an impact on many surely must create a difference between a... of those who drink the watermelon and thos...

To understand... one once said...

Surely if y... — in the G... near the bar... — you und...

whether your team had 26 points, as did mighty Georgia, or 21, as did almost as mighty Florida.

As a relative newcomer to this re-... will I feel cheated and ... saloons and ... ling again. Such pro-... tube.

Georgia-Florida games of the past could have offered any more. Even the weather cooperated.

If the game had a flaw it is that there was a loser.

Georgia loyalists will challenge such a statement, claiming to see an orange and blue gleam in my eyes that doesn't exist. And some Florida loyalists will insist on drowning their sorrows by telling themselves it was the same old story of Georgia defeating Florida when the game meant so much to the Gators.

But football purists and those who enjoy fine entertainment for entertainment's sake surely must agree with me. And you can bet ABC-TV...

who played and coached in it.

To forget this chapter of athletic history is beyond my comprehension.

From Georgia's point of view, it may be the day the No. 2-ranked Bulldogs won a national championship, getting an unexpected hand from their in-state rival, Georgia Tech, which tied top-ranked Notre Dame 3-3.

Then there was freshman running back Herschel Walker, clearly proving once again that he belongs in a class with few others. The game was three plays old when Walker sprinted right, broke several tackles and turned on his Olympic speed for a 72-yard touchdown run. He wasn't finished. Before the game was to end, Walker should have changed his name to Hercules. He ran 37 times for ... yards. He is amazing.

... most memorable

— Inside —
Georgia Florida '80

Georgia's winner wasn't fancy
... Page 10

Belue-to-Scott: The great heist
... Page 10

UF defenders say Walker not greatest
... Page 11

Sports

The Florida Times-Union
Jacksonville Journal
Sunday, November 9, 1980

Great Scott! A day for Dogs

Belue-to-Scott 93-yarder stops UF in thriller

By TOM CORNELISON
Journal Sports Writer

The Georgia Bulldogs were only ... to make a first down. They ... have won a national champion...

OCALA STAR-BANNER **sports**
Section **C**
SUNDAY, NOVEMBER 9, 1980

Georgia Miracle Nips Gators

By HERSCHEL NISSENSON
AP Sports Writer

JACKSONVILLE, Fla. (AP) — Herschel Walker, Georgia's fabulous freshman, shocked Florida with ... yard touchdo...

It was a heart-breaking loss for 6-2 Florida, which has made a dramatic turnaround from last season's 0-10 disaster.

College Clipboard
Georgia Tech Ties Notre Dame
See Notre Dame, page 6c

Here's how the Top Twenty...
The Associated Press foot...
listed and appeared:
1 Notre Dame (50-4) tied...
2-2
2 Georgia (11-0) beat Flo...
3 Florida State (10-1) bea...
Tech 31-4
4 Co California (7-0-1) bea...
23-14
5 Pittsburgh (9-0) beat Ba...
4-...
6 Ohio State (9-1) beat Ind...
7 UCLA (8-1) beat Washing...
8 Pittsburgh (9-1) beat Louisville...
23-...

ST. PETERSBURG TIMES **sports**
section **C**
SUNDAY, NOVEMBER 9, 1980

AGAIN! 'Dogs cost Gators so much

Clip and save Mizell column,
14-C (back-page)

By RAY HOLLIMAN
St. Petersburg Times Staff Writer

JACKSONVILLE — Georgia did it to Florida one more time Saturday.

Nothing fancy. Just a play the Bulldogs would have thought successful if it had gained 20 yards and allowed them to keep possession.

In fact, Florida coach Charley Pell called it "probably the simplest pass play in football."

But Georgia's Lindsay Scott turned the simplest pass play in football into a dramatic 93-yard touchdown with 1:03 left in the game to lift the Bulldogs from the precipice of their first loss of the season to a 26-21 victory over the Gators.

And, to make the day complete for Georgia, Scott's jaunt with the short pass from quarterback Buck Belue made the Bulldogs the only remaining team in the country with a perfect record. Georgia's fiercest rival, Georgia Tech, tied top-ranked Notre Dame 3-3, likely boosting the Bulldogs from No. 2 to No. 1 in the wire-service polls this week.

Plus, with only struggling Auburn remaining on the Southeastern Conference schedule, Georgia now is in command of the league race and just one win away from the Sugar Bowl berth that goes to the SEC champion.

AND FLORIDA — WELL, it's just another of the many blows the Gators have endured in the SEC races throughout history. Saturday, they had another chance.

With only 80 seconds remaining, it looked like their best chance ever. Had Florida beaten Georgia, it would have boosted the Gators into a tie for first place in the SEC with only a conference game against Kentucky remaining next week. As it is, Florida now is 6-2 overall, 3-2 ...

Gators so close but no cigar

SPORTS EDITOR
HUBERT MIZELL

JACKSONVILLE — No cigar. Unlike in recent Saturdays past, University of Florida football coach Charley Pell couldn't stand proud on a locker room trunk and flip victory stogies to his undergraduate smokers. And, for the 48th consecutive year, there will be no champagne toast over a Southeastern Conference championship trophy.

T-shirts told a tearful tale. Like Pell's cigars, those shirts ... a new-born Gator ...

drug the earth.

"All it was," said Pell, "was a simple curl (pattern). It might be the simplest pass in football. As Scott ran down the field, I kept thinking somebody would tackle him."

No tackle. No cigar.

Vince Dooley, the studious man who coaches Georgia football, is the Gators' master; there can be little doubting that. Dooley was a quite surprising hire as Bulldog head coach in 1964, for he had been but a freshman coach at Auburn. But this morning ... the Florida ...

20

"It was a special moment for all of us"

1980 GEORGIA BULLDOGS

First Row, L-R: Chuck Jones, Mark Malkiewicz, Jim Broadway, Richard Singleton, Rex Robinson, Mark McKay, Gary Cantrell, Head Coach Vince Dooley, Buck Belue, Dale Williams, Chris Welton, Matt Simon, John Lastinger, Pat Douglas. 2nd Row: Terry Hoage, Jeff Paulk, Tommy Lewis, Daryll Jones, Charlie Dean, Scott Woerner, Greg Bell, David Painter, Tim Bobo, Ronnie Stewart, Herschel Walker, Mike Jones, Chris McCarthy, Nate Taylor, Frank Ros, Jeff Hipp, Stan Dooley, Simmons, Bob Kelly, Scott Williams, Mike Fisher, Keith Middleton, Frederick Lamar, Wayne Radloff, Joe Happe, George Kesler, Larry Cage, Jack Lindsey, Tommy Thurson, Pat McShea. 4th Row: Will Forts, Keith Middleton, Frederick Lamar, Wayne Radloff, Joe Happe, George Kesler, Larry Cage, Jack Lindsey, Tommy Thurson, Charles Smith, Tommy Nix. 5th Row: Dan Leusenring, Hugh Nall, Wayne Radloff, Todd Milton, Nat Hudson, Jeff Harper, Tim Morrison, Jim Blakewood, Winford Eddie Weaver. 6th Row: Harold Malloy, Mike Weaver, Scott Campbell, Tim Case, Marty Ballard, Guy McIntyre, Jimmy Harper, James Brown, Guy Stargell, Jimmy Jay McAlister. 7th Row: Keith Cannon, Kevin Jackson, Tim Case, Marty Ballard, Arp Arnold, Robert Miles, Clarence Kay, Joe Creamons, Keith Bouchillon, Dale Carver. Hood, Mac Thompson, Roy Curtis. 8th Row: Charles Junior, Lon Buckler, Dan Marlow, Warren Gray, Joe Creamons, Keith Bouchillon, Dale Carver. Payne, Norris Brown, Eric Jarvis. 9th Row: Freddie Gilbert, Tim Crowe, Dan Marlow, Warren Gray, Keith Hall, Tim Parks, Landy Ewings.

Two days later, it became official. Georgia was seated atop the, albeit, unsteady throne of college football for the first time in 38 years. The Bulldogs were the third squad to move into that revolving penthouse suite in less than a month joining Alabama and Notre Dame as renters.

But, Vince Dooley's canines did not want their visit to be a short, weekend vacation. Rather, their goal was to make the penthouse a home for the remainder of the 1980 season.

"As a football fan and particularly as a Georgia fan I am very excited about it (being No. 1)," Dooley said. "The polls are great for the game of football and great for the fans and really great for the Georgia fans today.

"But, as a football coach and particularly as the Georgia football coach I don't like weekly polls, particularly because of the history of the last two weekly No. 1's. The significant thing about us being No. 1 is that we have not lost yet. The only poll I'm really concerned with is the one in January. That's what it's all about."

Meanwhile, Florida's coaching staff had more pieces to put back together than "All the King's horses, And all the King's men" did with Humpty Dumpty. Charley Pell, though, was confident in his charges.

"I believe we have the type of players that can come back from this," he said.

The following week, focus, not the opponents themselves was the greater challenge for each team. The Gators were prey to "What might have been" and the Dogs to "What might be."

THE ATLANTA CONSTITUTION

Morning Sports 2 NBA 3
For The Record 2 Preps 8

Sports

SECTION D

····· Tuesday, November 11, 1980 ···

Georgia Rated No. 1 By UPI
Southern Cal Ranks Second, Nebraska Third, Florida State Fourth

Florida did regroup. Trailing 15-14 late against Kentucky in Lexington, Wayne Peace did what he was unable to do against Georgia, engineer a late come-from-behind victory.

Gator place kicker Brian Clark, who had his moment in the sun eclipsed by Lindsay Scott a week before, shined bright against the Wildcats as he booted the game winning field goal with six seconds left to give Florida a gutsy 17-15 win and a bid to the Tangerine Bowl.

"We knew that the thing that would make the difference this week is what the players had inside," Pell said. "I think you saw a glimpse of that today. We wanted to show today what the Gators of 1980 have inside."

On the outside, Georgia was looking to remove the albatross, Auburn, that had hung around its neck in 1978 and 1979. The Bulldogs had faced the Tigers both years with an SEC title and Sugar Bowl birth on the line. Twice, Sugar Bowl officials breathed a sigh of relief as Auburn halted Georgia's dreams enabling Alabama to play for and win consecutive national crowns in New Orleans.

The Bulldogs were still four quarters away from its own trip to the Crescent City and found themselves trailing 7-3 in the second quarter. Once again Georgia's cavalry, its special teams, came riding in to the rescue. Senior Chris Welton blocked an Auburn punt, and Freddie Gilbert returned it for a touchdown. The play gave Georgia a 10-7 lead and ignited a run of 28 unanswered points.

When the clock ran out at Jordan-Hare Stadium, the No. 1 team in the nation stayed that way with a 31-21 victory on The Plains and clinched the fourth SEC championship in Dooley's 17-year tenure in Athens. The Bulldogs accepted a bid to the Sugar Bowl to play Notre Dame.

> Georgia still had one final hurdle to jump that would guarantee it the opportunity to play for the national championship. The Bulldogs made sure they would not suffer the same fate as the Fighting Irish and finished off in-state rival Georgia Tech, 38-20, in Sanford Stadium.

"Today our seniors made up for the last three years," Vince Dooley said.

Georgia still had one final hurdle to jump that would guarantee it the opportunity to play for the national championship. The Bulldogs made sure they would not suffer the same fate as the Fighting Irish and finished off in-state rival Georgia Tech 38-20 in Sanford Stadium. To top the regular season off, Herschel Walker set a new NCAA freshman rushing record against Tech, breaking Tony Dorsett's old mark.

The Gators stumbled in their last two games losing to Sunshine State rivals Miami (31-7) at home and hated Florida State (17-13) in Tallahassee.

In the post-season, the Bulldogs and Gators both completed amazing campaigns. In only two years, Pell had resurrected the Florida program from an also-ran to a viable, SEC contender. The Gators overpowered Maryland 35-20 for a Tangerine Bowl win to finish 8-4 and had their sights on the future.

"The cool part is you look back on the history of it," Wayne Peace said. "That kind of showed the Florida

1980 GEORGIA BULLDOGS SEC CHAMPS NATIONAL CHAMPIONS #1

people and the Florida team that the program was going in the right direction. There would be better things ahead."

The New Year in New Orleans, La. began with a new addition to Georgia's storied football history - its first-ever national championship. The Bulldogs claimed their crown with a 17-10 victory over Notre Dame in the Super Dome and finished as the only unbeaten team in college football.

A generation has passed since Georgia claimed the 1980 national title. But, for those who experienced the magical five-month journey, the epicenter will always be found in Jacksonville.

"I'm sure that 95%-98% of the Bulldog nation would tell you that Belue to Scott is the greatest play in Georgia's history," Dooley said. "I've said that and still believe it because not only did it win that football game, but what it eventually led to was the only undisputed, undefeated national championship team at Georgia."

"In my mind, that's the most important call Larry (Munson) has ever had," Tony Barnhart said, "and the most important play in the history of Georgia football."

For Joe Happe, November 8, 1980 almost feels like yesterday.

"It's hard to believe it's been almost 30 years," he reflected. "I can close my eyes and I can see the field, feel the field. It was a very bright day and it's hard to believe. The memories, they carry on. They carry on for all of us. It was a special moment for all of us."

For those on the opposite sideline, the wound has not completely healed.

"It is hard to swallow to this day," Robin Fisher said. "It is. We came back from a 0-10-1 season the year before to have a really good year at 8-4 with a lot on the line. Had we won that ballgame, we would have had a great year. We fell about 93 seconds short of possibly one of the best turn around seasons in all of college sports."

"If somebody were to ask me what game hurts the most that you lost, definitely it was that game, absolutely," Peace said, "Florida had never won an SEC title. If we beat Georgia that day, we had a great chance of winning it. A lot of things could have happened that day."

Mike Bugar, now the defensive coordinator at Texas State University, said Scott's gallop to glory radiated after-shocks in future meetings.

"I was there for three years, '80, '81 and '82," he recalled, "and I really believe the way we lost the 1980 game had an effect the next couple of years we played

Georgia. For the guys who played in the game, there was always a doubt in their minds because of the way we lost."

Each year, members of that Gator team are annually reminded of the heartache.

"ESPN Classic shows it every year," Fisher said. "Every year I get a call from somebody saying, 'Fish, I'm watching you on TV. It's the Florida-Georgia game.' I say, 'Yeah, I know. They're playing that damn thing again.'

"I've never been in the spot where I could sit down and watch it, but I don't think it would be hard to watch. I'm not bitter about it. I think I gave it all that day. It just wasn't good enough to the win. It's one of those days you don't get the chance to forget."

Tim Groves, the Florida safety who made a final, desperation dive at Scott's feet, gets an ear full every year at his oyster bar, the Thirsty Gator, in Winter Park, Fl.

"It's something that has haunted me for a long time," he said. "I get reminded about it every year watching that replay on TV. To this day there will be people who have been Gator fans their whole life say to me, 'Timmy, you're a slow, white boy.' I say, 'Listen guys, I'm not ever going to catch him, never, ever going to catch him. There's nothing I can do to change it. It'll never change."

The play and the moment forever changed the lives of those involved.

"The legacy for me is things get tough, difficult and people make mistakes," Lindsay Scott said, "but the way you handle it is to do the next right thing. Life isn't a piece of cake and I've been able to learn from that situation."

Dock Luckie took the negative outcome and has tried to turn it into a positive.

"Lindsay Scott, he instilled a lot of stuff inside of me," Luckie said. "One of these days, I would like to meet him, shake his hand and congratulate him personally and let him know what he did that day has enabled me to teach my son and a lot of other athletes to don't quit until it's over. Hopefully, they will catch it and run for victory. That's what Lindsay Scott did."

MEMORIES

Mike Bugar, Florida defensive line coach, 1980-1982

"There ain't but one memory from that game, 93 yards and a touchdown with a minute left to go in the game by Lindsay Scott."

Joe Happe, Georgia center

"It's an integral part of my life. The whole experience, that whole year, not so much the game, has helped shape who I am and how I go about things."

Claude Felton, Georgia sports information director

"Without that play, there's no national championship. You can go back and say without Herschel Walker coming on against Tennessee, and if South Carolina doesn't fumble at the end of the game they at least tie or win that game. Anytime you have a season like that, you can always look back and say here are three cases the ball bounced right and we were lucky to pull it out."

Sonny Seiler, '56 Georgia alumnus, owner of Uga

"It was a wonderful, wonderful occasion engineered by two of the best players we've ever had. What a wonderful experience it was not only to beat Florida but also to beat them on the way to the national championship."

> **"The next day, when I got ready to check out of the hotel, I told the manager I had destroyed his lamp. He looked at me and said, 'Sir, let me get this straight. You destroyed the lamp while pulling against Florida?' I said, 'That's right.' He didn't make me pay for it. He was a Florida State fan."**
>
> — *Tony Barnhart, CBS Sports*

Sheila Hoeppner, '83 Georgia alumnus

"Even after all these years, it absolutely does stick with me. I still cannot hear the Munson clip without getting chills up my spine. There is nothing like that warm wonderful feeling knowing that I witnessed something pretty special that afternoon."

Bucky Cook, '77 Georgia alumnus

"I don't know whether God actually participates in the outcome of athletic events, but if he does, that day he was certainly a Bulldog."

Murray Poole, former sports editor Brunswick News

"The Georgia-Florida game in 1980 is always about Buck and Lindsay, and rightfully so because they made the biggest play in Georgia history. If it had not been for that freshman Herschel Walker, they would not have been in that position to make that play. It wouldn't have been as close as it was in those last few seconds."

Bob Wolcott, '84 Georgia alumnus

"It was my first Georgia-Florida game. I had such a great time golfing at Jekyll Island in the Georgia-Florida Golf Classic. I remember the perfect weather, the parties were second to none, beach music everywhere and everyone wearing their favorite colors. Then, to go to the game, come over the bridge and watch the teams arrive was electric."

Bobby Gaston, former SEC official

"Over 25 years of officiating, I worked 10-11 games a year and six national championship games. I don't know if I've ever seen a play cause that much emotion. It's one in a million."

Robin Fisher, Florida nose guard

"You hear those coaches tell you, 'You'll remember this the rest of your life.' When you're a 20 year old, you go, 'Yeah coach, right.' But, it's amazing how that game has stuck with me all my life."

Karin Koser, '81 Georgia alumnus

"It ranks right up there with seeing Prince Charles visit (to Sanford Stadium in 1977); winning the National Championship and having Herschel (Walker) buy me soap which I used with a friend to soap a girl's car who had temporarily stolen her boyfriend."

Dock Luckie, Florida defensive tackle

"I learned a lot from that game for life. No matter where I go, I really focus on the task and never let my guard down till its over. Before I go to sleep, I leave one eye open before I close the other one because I want to make sure everything is alright."

"You're going to the game."

Carl Brantley, Georgia fan

"Three days before the game, my father had a heart attack. I went to Savannah and he said, 'I'm glad you came, what time are you leaving for Jacksonville? ' I said, 'I'm not going to the game dad, you've had a heart attack and you're in intensive care.' He said, 'You're going to the game. We don't miss this game.' I said, 'O.K., I'll go.'

"I was going to rush back because I wanted to relieve my brother and I was supposed to tell dad about the game. I didn't know this until later, but during the game, my brother slips one of those cheap little battery powered radios into intensive care. He turned the radio on during the game, and on that play, dad got so excited, his heart rate started going crazy. The nurse ran in and threw my brother out. She told daddy he had to calm down. Dad is pretty much saying, 'You're not going to tell me to shut up until this game is over. I've got to know if we win...'

"After 45 minutes to get out of the stands and another hour or so to get out of the parking lot, I finally got back to the hospital. At that time, you could go into intensive care every couple of hours for like 10-15 minutes. I go in there and dad is asleep. I patted him on his wrist, and he opened up his eyes. Dad had these really cold, steel blue eyes and he said, 'How bout' them Dawgs?' He said tell me about the game. I said, 'Dad, I can't tell you in five or 10 minutes.' The nurse came in and he said, 'Let my boy stay, I've got to hear about this game.'

"At the time, I lived in Athens and worked at Belk department store. Some of the players and Erk Russell used to come in and buy clothes. A couple of

Top: Thom Brantley, T.D. Brantley, and Carl Brantley. Below: A "Get Well" card sent to T.D. Brantley and signed by UGA coaches and players.

them became good friends of mine and I told them about my dad. The week after the game, they got a get well card, signed it and sent it to my father.

"When my father died in 1995, he was 71. In the will, he said that card went to me because of how much it meant. The card is in my safety deposit box in Colorado Springs, Colo. Every year, I take it out, and I look at it before I go to meet Tony Barnhart at the Georgia-Florida game. That card always reminds me that 1980 was so special. To this day, I can always relate that game not just to what I experienced, but how my dad experienced it through me while laying in a hospital bed."

Appendix

FINAL GAME STATS

Team	Georgia	Florida
Score	26	21
First Downs	17	20
Rushes-Yardage (Net)	53-286	42-123
Passing-Yardage (Net)	145	286
Return Yardage (Net)	29	24
Passes-Att.-Comp.-Int.	16-7-2	37-20-2
Total Offense-Yards	431	409
Punts (Number-Average)	5-46.2	7-35.1
Fumbles-Lost	3-2	2-1
Penalties-Yards	5-45	8-99

Individual Leaders

Georgia (Visitors)

Rushing	Att.	Net Yards	TD	Long
Herschel Walker	37	235	1	72
Buck Belue	9	26		
Jimmy Womack	5	18		

Passing	Att-Comp-Int.	Yds	TD
Buck Belue	16-7-2	145	1

Pass Receiving	No.	Yards	TD	Long
Lindsay Scott	2	144	1	93
Ronnie Stewart	1	13		1

Punting	No.	Avg.	Long
Mark Malkiewicz	5	46.2	57

Florida (Home)

Rushing	Att.	Net Yards	TD	Long
James Jones	22	89	1	12
Wayne Peace	12	13		
Cris Collinsworth	2	12		

Passing	Att-Comp-Int.	Yds	TD
Wayne Peace	37-20-2	286	1

Pass Receiving	No.	Yards	TD	Long
Cris Collinsworth	3	29	1	13
Tyrone Young	10	183		54
Spencer Jackson	3	23		12

Punting	No.	Avg.	Long
Mark Dickert	7	35.1	43

Official Scoring Summary

Georgia vs Florida

Date: 11-8-80
Site: Gator Bowl, Jacksonville, Fla.
Attendance: 68,528

Score by Quarters	1	2	3	4	Final
Georgia	7	7	6	6	26
Florida	3	7	0	11	21

1st Quarter
GA: Herschel Walker 72 Run (Rex Robinson kick), 13:09
FLA: Brian Clark FG 40, 7:07

2nd Quarter
GA: Ronnie Stewart 13 pass from Buck Belue (Robinson kick), 13:39
FLA: Cris Collinsworth 9 pass from Wayne Peace (Clark kick), 7:10

3rd Quarter
GA: Robinson FG 24, 9:38
GA: Robinson FG 20, 3:58

4th Quarter
GA: James Jones 11 run (Tyrone Young pass from Peace), 14:14
FLA: Clark FG 40, 6:52
GA: Lindsay Scott 93 pass from Belue (Belue pass failed), 1:03

Defensive Statistics

Georgia

Tackles	UT	AT	Tot
Frank Ros	4	6	10
Nate Taylor	2	8	10
1 pass break up			
Tommy Thurson	1	7	8
Eddie Weaver	2	6	8
1 fumble recovered			
Jimmy Payne	3	4	7
14 yards in tackles for loss			
Tim Crowe	1	5	6
4 yards in tackles for loss			
Jeff Hipp	4	1	5
2 pass break ups			
Chris Welton	3	2	5
Tim McShea	1	4	5
Mike Fisher	2	3	5
2 interceptions			
Tim Bobo	2	2	4
Scott Woerner	1	2	3
Tim Carver	1	1	2

Florida

Tackles	UT	AT	Tot
David Little	6	11	17
Fernando Jackson	4	13	17
Tim Golden	3	4	7
David Galloway	3	3	6
Kyle Knight	1	4	51
1 fumbled recovered			
Val Brown	2	2	4
Ron Coleman	2	2	4
Ivory Curry	1	2	3
1 pass intercepted (22 yard net return)			
Doc Luckie	0	2	2
Vito McKever	1	1	2
1 pass intercepted and broken up			
John Whittaker	1	1	2
Tim Groves	0	2	2
2 pass break ups			
Tom Weigmann	0	1	1
Sonny Gilliam	0	1	1
1 fumble recovered			
Mike Clark	0	1	1

Tommy Thurson and Eddie Weaver turn this Gator into Dawg food.

FLORIDA GATORS ROSTER*

No.	Name	Position	Height	Weight	Class	No.	Name	Position	Height	Weight	Class
1	Dale Dorminey	QB	6-1	186	Fr.	53	Rod Brooks	DE	6-0	214	Sr.
3	Brian Clark	PK	6-2	192	Jr.	54	Van Jones	DT	6-5	233	Jr.
4	Mark Dickert	P	5-10	161	Jr.	56	Ryan Fraser	OL	6-2	238	So.
5	Jim Gainey	PK	6-1	176	So.	57	Tim Golden	DE	6-1	224	Sr.
6	Charlie Kerr	DB	6-5	212	Fr.	58	Ray Lawrence	C	6-3	225	Sr.
10	Tyrone Young	WR	6-6	184	So.	59	Doug Smith	C	6-2	230	So.
14	Johnell Brown	RB	5-10	192	So.	62	John Whittaker	NG	6-1	240	Jr.
15	Wayne Peace	QB	6-2	211	Fr.	63	Lawrence Patrick	DE	6-2	226	So.
16	Roger Sibbaid	QB	6-0	190	Fr.	65	Dan Plonk	OL	6-2	244	So.
17	Mark Massey	QB	6-1	177	Fr.	66	Robin Fisher	NG	6-0	229	Jr.
18	Tony Lilly	DB	6-1	188	Fr.	67	Val Brown	DE	6-4	228	So.
20	Tim Groves	DB	6-2	198	Sr.	69	Dan Fike	OL	6-6	256	So.
21	Cris Collinsworth	WR	6-4	192	Sr.	70	Joe Wickline	OL	6-3	260	Sr.
23	Gordon Pleasants	DB	6-1	213	So.	71	Jim Kalamaras	LB	5-10	209	So.
24	Kyle Knight	DB	5-9	178	So.	72	Dock Luckie	DT	6-2	262	Sr.
26	Ivory Curry	DB	5-11	180	So.	73	Buddy Schultheis	OL	6-5	245	Fr.
27	David Norwood	DB	6-2	193	Fr.	74	Wally Hough	OL	6-3	263	Sr.
28	Curt Garrett	WR	6-0	191	Jr.	75	Jim Subers	OL	6-4	248	Sr.
30	James Jones	FB	6-2	233	So.	77	John Redmond	C	6-3	237	So.
31	Terry Williams	FB	5-11	201	Sr.	79	Jon Moyle	OL	6-4	239	Fr.
32	Doug Kellom	RB	5-8	180	So.	80	Chris Faulkner	TE	6-5	248	So.
33	Calvin Davis	FB	5-9	199	Jr.	82	Mike Mularkey	TE	6-3	235	So.
36	Vito McKeever	DB	5-11	174	Fr.	83	Dwayne Dixon	WR	6-1	202	Fr.
39	Carl Prioleau	RB	5-7	189	Sr.	85	David Galloway	DT	6-3	266	Jr.
41	Larry Keefe	DE	6-2	193	So.	86	Vince Jones	DT	6-6	256	So.
42	Sonny Gilliam	DB	5-9	176	So.	87	Mike Clark	DT	6-4	241	Sr.
44	Derald Williams	RB	5-11	204	So.	88	Wilber Marshall	TE	6-0	220	Fr.
45	Mike Ricketts	LB	5-11	218	So.	89	Spencer Jackson	WR	5-11	178	So.
46	Fred McCallister	LB	6-0	227	Fr.	91	John Landry	LB	6-0	214	Fr.
47	Bruce Vaughan	DB	5-11	165	So.	92	Ron Coleman	DT	6-4	252	Sr.
48	Doug Drew	DB	5-11	178	So.	94	Pete Garcia	LB	5-10	208	So.
49	Fernando Jackson	LB	5-11	207	So.	95	Tom Wiegmann	LB	6-1	218	So.
51	David Little	LB	6-1	228	Sr.	99	Roy Harris	DT	6-3	250	Fr.
52	Phil Pharr	C	6-2	218	Sr.						

*These are the team Rosters as they appeared in the official game program

GEORGIA BULLDOGS ROSTER*

No.	Name	Position	Height	Weight	Class	No.	Name	Position	Height	Weight	Class
1	Chuck Jones	WR	6-0	198	So.	47	Nate Taylor	LB	5-11	198	So.
2	Mark Malkiewicz	P	6-2	200	Sr.	48	Frank Ros	LB	6-1	215	Sr.
3	Jim Broadway	P	5-10	170	So.	49	Jeff Hipp	S	6-3	190	Sr.
5	Rex Robinson	PK	6-0	205	Sr.	51	Robert Arthur	C	6-1	209	
8	Buck Belue	QB	6-1	188	Jr.	52	Tommy Nix	C	6-2	190	Sr.
9	Dale Williams	CB	6-0	165	Jr.	53	Dan Leusenring	OG	6-3	240	So.
10	Chris Welton	FS	6-1	190	Sr.	55	Wayne Radloff	C	6-5	252	So.
11	Matt Simon	TB	6-0	185	Jr.	56	Joe Happe	C	6-3	240	So.
12	John Lastinger	QB	6-2	190	So.	57	George Kesler	C	6-1	195	Sr.
14	Terry Hoage	DB	6-3	196	Fr.	59	Jack Lindsey	DT	6-2	232	So.
15	Jeff Paulk	QB	6-1	185	So.	60	Tommy Thurson	LB	6-2	207	Fr.
17	Daryll Jones	QB	6-1	192	Fr.	61	Eddie Weaver	DG	6-1	264	Jr.
18	Charlie Dean	S	6-1	175	Fr.	65	Nat Hudson	OG	6-3	265	Sr.
19	Scott Woerner	CB	6-0	188	Sr.	66	Jeff Harper	OT	6-3	245	Sr.
20	Greg Bell	CB	5-11	187	Sr.	68	Warren Gray	OG	6-3	239	Fr.
22	David Palmer	SE	6-2	180	So.	71	Kavin Jackson	DG	6-2	242	So.
23	Steve Kelly	CB	5-9	172	Jr.	72	Tim Case	OT	6-4	245	So.
24	Lindsay Scott	SE	6-1	188	Jr.	75	Jimmy Harper	OT	6-5	284	Fr.
25	Jimmy Womack	FB	5-10	205	Sr.	76	Tim Morrison	OG	6-3	254	Sr.
26	Stan Charping	CB	5-9	190	So.	77	Jim Blakewood	OT	6-2	247	Jr.
27	Donnie McMickens	TB	5-11	205	Sr.	78	Winford Hood	OT	6-3	259	Fr.
29	Bob Kelly	S	5-11	172	Sr.	80	Charles Junior	SE	6-3	175	So.
31	Mike Fisher	CB	6-0	173	Sr.	82	Amp Arnold	FL	6-0	175	Sr.
32	Tim Bobo	DE	6-2	210	So.	83	Robert Miles	DE	6-1	230	Sr.
33	Ronnie Stewart	FB	5-10	205	Jr.	84	Clarence Kay	TE	6-3	215	Fr.
34	Herschel Walker	TB	6-1	218	Fr.	86	Guy Stargell	TE	6-1	215	So.
36	Carnie Norris	TB	5-9	185	So.	87	Jimmy Payne	DT	6-4	238	So.
37	Paul Frate	PK	5-10	155	So.	88	Norris Brown	TE	6-3	220	So.
38	Barry Young	TB	6-2	225	Fr.	90	Freddie Gilbert	DE	6-4	213	Fr.
41	Pat McShea	DE	6-2	220	Sr.	91	Tim Crowe	DG	6-1	230	So.
42	Will Forts	LB	6-0	207	So.	94	Joe Creamons	DG	6-2	235	Jr.
43	Keith Middleton	LB	6-1	213	Sr.	95	Keith Bouchillon	DE	6-2	205	Jr.
45	Mike Jones	LB	6-1	192	Fr.	96	Dale Carver	DE	6-2	225	So.
46	Chris McCarthy	FB	5-11	205	So.	98	Tim Parks	DG	6-3	242	Sr.

CHRONOLOGY OF GEORGIA VS. FLORIDA
Georgia leads 47-38-2

Year	Result	Score	Location
1904	Won	52-0	Macon, Ga.
1915	Won	39-0	Jacksonville, Fla.
1916	Won	21-0	Athens, Ga.
1919	Won	16-0	Tampa, Fla.
1920	Won	56-0	Athens, Ga.
1926	Won	32-9	Athens, Ga.
1927	Won	28-0	Jacksonville, Fla.
1928	Lost	6-26	Savannah, Ga.
1929	Lost	6-18	Jacksonville, Fla.
1930	Tie	0-0	Savannah, Ga.
1931	Won	33-6	Gainesville, Fla.
1932	Won	33-12	Athens, Ga.
1933	Won	14-0	Jacksonville, Fla.
1934	Won	14-0	Jacksonville, Fla.
1935	Won	7-0	Jacksonville, Fla.
1936	Won	26-8	Jacksonville, Fla.
1937	Lost	0-6	Jacksonville, Fla.
1938	Won	19-6	Jacksonville, Fla.
1939	Won	6-2	Jacksonville, Fla.
1940	Lost	12-18	Jacksonville, Fla.
1941	Won	19-3	Jacksonville, Fla.
1942	Won	75-0	Jacksonville, Fla.
1944	Won	38-12	Jacksonville, Fla.
1945	Won	34-0	Jacksonville, Fla.
1946	Won	33-14	Jacksonville, Fla.
1947	Won	34-6	Jacksonville, Fla.
1948	Won	20-12	Jacksonville, Fla.
1949	Lost	7-28	Jacksonville, Fla.
1950	Won	6-0	Jacksonville, Fla.
1951	Won	7-6	Jacksonville, Fla.
1952	Lost	0-30	Jacksonville, Fla.
1953	Lost	7-21	Jacksonville, Fla.
1954	Won	14-13	Jacksonville, Fla.
1955	Lost	13-19	Jacksonville, Fla.
1956	Lost	0-28	Jacksonville, Fla.
1957	Lost	0-22	Jacksonville, Fla.
1958	Lost	6-7	Jacksonville, Fla.
1959	Won	21-10	Jacksonville, Fla.
1960	Lost	14-22	Jacksonville, Fla.
1961	Lost	14-21	Jacksonville, Fla.
1962	Lost	15-23	Jacksonville, Fla.
1963	Lost	14-21	Jacksonville, Fla.
1964	Won	14-7	Jacksonville, Fla.
1965	Lost	10-14	Jacksonville, Fla.
1966	Won	27-10	Jacksonville, Fla.
1967	Lost	16-17	Jacksonville, Fla.
1968	Won	51-0	Jacksonville, Fla.
1969	Tie	13-13	Jacksonville, Fla.
1970	Lost	17-24	Jacksonville, Fla.
1971	Won	49-7	Jacksonville, Fla.
1972	Won	10-7	Jacksonville, Fla.
1973	Lost	10-11	Jacksonville, Fla.
1974	Won	17-16	Jacksonville, Fla.
1975	Won	10-7	Jacksonville, Fla.
1976	Won	41-27	Jacksonville, Fla.
1977	Lost	17-22	Jacksonville, Fla.
1978	Won	24-22	Jacksonville, Fla.
1979	Won	33-10	Jacksonville, Fla.
1980	Won	26-21	Jacksonville, Fla.
1981	Won	26-21	Jacksonville, Fla.
1982	Won	44-0	Jacksonville, Fla.
1983	Won	10-9	Jacksonville, Fla.
1984	Lost	0-27	Jacksonville, Fla.
1985	Won	24-3	Jacksonville, Fla.
1986	Lost	19-31	Jacksonville, Fla.
1987	Won	23-10	Jacksonville, Fla.
1988	Won	26-3	Jacksonville, Fla.
1989	Won	17-10	Jacksonville, Fla.
1990	Lost	7-38	Jacksonville, Fla.
1991	Lost	13-45	Jacksonville, Fla.
1992	Lost	24-26	Jacksonville, Fla.
1993	Lost	26-33	Jacksonville, Fla.
1994	Lost	14-52	Gainesville, Fla.
1995	Lost	17-52	Athens, Ga.
1996	Lost	7-47	Jacksonville, Fla.
1997	Won	37-17	Jacksonville, Fla.
1998	Lost	7-38	Jacksonville, Fla.
1999	Lost	14-30	Jacksonville, Fla.
2000	Lost	23-34	Jacksonville, Fla.
2001	Lost	10-24	Jacksonville, Fla.
2002	Lost	13-20	Jacksonville, Fla.
2003	Lost	13-16	Jacksonville, Fla.
2004	Won	31-24	Jacksonville, Fla.
2005	Lost	10-14	Jacksonville, Fla.
2006	Lost	14-21	Jacksonville, Fla.
2007	Won	42-30	Jacksonville, Fla.
2008	Lost	10-49	Jacksonville, Fla.
2009	Lost	17-41	Jacksonville, Fla.
Totals		**1718-1388**	

Record at Home: 4-1-0
Record at Sanford Stadium: 1-1-0
Record at Gainesville: 1-1-0
Record at Florida Field: 1-1-0
Record at Jacksonville: 40-37-1
Record at Neutral Sites: 42-34-2
Games Decided by seven points or less: 15-17-2
Longest Winning Streak: 7 (1941-48; 1904-27)
Longest Losing Streak (7; 1990-96)
Last 10 meetings: 2-8
Biggest win: 75 (75-0 in 1942)
Biggest Loss: 40 (7-47 in 1996)